REGIONS OF CAPTIVITY

REGIONS OF CAPTIVITY

One of the Most Powerful Ways to Be Delivered

Dr. Ana Méndez Ferrell

DESTINY IMAGE® PUBLISHERS, INC.

P.O. Box 310, Shippensburg, PA 17257-0310

"Speaking to the Purposes of God for this Generation and for the Generations to Come."

Previously published as Regions of Captivity by Voice of Light Ministries copyright 2009
ISBN 978-1-933-163-22-2

This book and all other Destiny Image, Revival Press, MercyPlace, Fresh Bread, Destiny Image Fiction, and Treasure House books are available at Christian bookstores and distributors worldwide.

For a U.S. bookstore nearest you, call **1-800-722-6774.**

For more information on foreign distributors, call **717-532-3040.**

Or reach us on the Internet: **www.destinyimage.com.**

Trade Paper ISBN 13: 978-0-7684-3233-6

Hardcover ISBN 13: 978-0-7684-3420-0

Large Print ISBN 13: 978-0-7684-3421-7

E-book ISBN 13: 978-0-7684-9306-1

For Worldwide Distribution, Printed in the U.S.A.

1 2 3 4 5 6 7 8 9 10 11 / 13 12 11 10

Dedication

I dedicate this book to my heavenly Father, to my beloved Jesus, to the Holy Spirit, and to all the brave deliverers around the world who have paid the price to see captive souls set free.

Endorsements

Do not only read this book, let these truths set you free.

In the few years that I have known Sister Ana Méndez Ferrell and her husband, Brother Emerson Ferrell, I have seen their commitment to pay the price to see people set free through faith in Jesus Christ.

I recognize through experience that the revelations in this book only come to someone from God through trial and hardship. The words given here are part of what God wants the Church to understand: it is through spiritual warfare and sacrifice of personal comfort that we will see souls set free.

I have personally heard Sister Ana teach this message and have seen the freedom that comes through its application to hurting people. You will not accomplish what God has ready for your life if there are areas that remain in captivity.

—David L. Hogan
Founder and President
Freedom Ministries
Mexico/USA

Now, as never before, the Body of Christ needs to move up a notch in its knowledge and application of the principles of serious spiritual warfare.

No one knows this better than Ana Méndez Ferrell who has been an inside player on both sides of the conflict.

In *Regions of Captivity*, Ana gives us new and valuable insights which, if used with discretion under the power of the Holy Spirit, can measurably hasten the defeat of the enemy and accelerate the advance of the Kingdom of God.

—C. Peter Wagner
Presiding Apostle, International Coalition of Apostles
President, Global Harvest Ministries
Chancellor, Wagner Leadership Institute
Colorado Springs, Colorado, USA

I have known Prophetess Ana Méndez Ferrell since the beginning of her ministry. I have been her mentor, pastor, and spiritual father for almost 15 years. She is, without a doubt, an extremely brave woman. Therefore, the topic that she brings forth in this book defies conventional theology. She boldly examines this topic, knowing that it will stir up some negative responses.

However, it will also bring forth positive reactions, especially from leaders and ministers who have had experiences similar to hers. They have been hoping for a book like this to encourage them so they can continue the work of setting captives free from the schemes of hell.

This material should be read with humility, prayer, fasting, and praise. Enjoy it, beloved reader. I recommend it. It will change your perspective of your service to God and to the prisoners of darkness.

—Apostle Dr. Rony Chaves
Founder and President,
Ministerio Avance Misionero Mundial and
La Red Apostólica Latino Americana RAMCU
San José, Costa Rica

I thank God for the life of Prophetess Ana Méndez Ferrell. Personally, I believe that she is one of the most powerful warriors in the Body of

Christ today. She doesn't just talk about spiritual warfare—she lives it. I have witnessed some of her encounters with enemy forces and must say she is one of the most used prophets of our time in the area of spiritual warfare.

This book deals with regions of captivity in which this prophetess is an expert. She describes different regions of captivity and their locations. She also explains Jesus' role in setting captive souls free and shares the revelation and the steps to freedom. There are many theoretical books, but they don't teach you how to apply their knowledge. However, Ana presents practical tools for those who want to live in freedom. I personally recommend this book to every Christian, as each revelation is backed up by the Word of God. Also, the testimonies included here will help people who are still satan's captives in different areas. The anointing of God is on this work to fulfill Jesus' purpose of setting people free from the captivity of homosexuality, drug addiction, alcohol, sickness, and more. It doesn't matter what the problem is—this book will bless you.

—Apostle Guillermo Maldonado
El Rey Jesús Church
Miami, Florida, USA

For several years in the ministry, we observed how people, although they professed of having accepted Christ as Lord and Savior, continued suffering from innumerable situations such as depression, oppression, obsession, and even demon possession. It was painful to see how these people endured insults and continual injustices and persecutions. With every incident, they seemed to sink deeper into a hole with no way out.

Bless God for allowing Prophetess Ana Méndez Ferrell to experience the places of captivity mentioned in the Bible. Many generations have been trapped there and Ana was shown how to minister deliverance to these captive souls. We have applied these revelations recently while ministering deliverance to captives. It has brought us great joy to see souls taken from those prisons of darkness and begin to enjoy a new life. Without a doubt, this book is a powerful tool for every minister who, like us, desires to see souls set free and enjoying abundant life in Christ. *Hallelujah!*

—Apostles Alex and Rosy Funes
Ministerio Apostólico Avance Misionero
Jacksonville, Florida, USA

Upon reading in Isaiah 61 that Jesus came to set the captives free, I always interpreted it as referring to people who were demon possessed. However, the Lord was telling the Church that there is a way to open places where people have been held captive. Then we began to open prisons in which many of our young people and adults were captive.

I discovered the difference that this made in people's deliverance and inner healing. We were able to set many people free from the places where they were being held captive. One of them was a man whose demons continually manifested for two consecutive years. When we set him free from his spiritual prisons, he found his true freedom.

We received this same revelation from the Lord. I was thrilled to see that Ana Méndez Ferrell was doing the same thing in Mexico that we were teaching by the Holy Spirit in Brazil. However, I must admit that Ana has received more revelation as far as the regions of captivity are concerned. This book is going to help people who are in the ministry of deliverance to go deeper in this subject.

Today, I could not develop my ministry of deliverance without taking into consideration people's captivity in order to truly set them free.

—Apostle Neuza Itioka
Sao Paulo, Brazil

Contents

Foreword

The restoration of apostolic and prophetic ministries has opened the way for greater revelation to be released to the Church worldwide. God is opening up the Spirit realm and pioneers are helping us enter into new realms of understanding. The revelation contained in this book has a pioneering thrust to set the captives free.

I have always desired to see people set free through the power of the Holy Spirit. I have read many books on the subject over the years, but nothing has come into my hands as unique as this. The content of this book is new and fresh. The revelation will expand your understanding of deliverance and give you greater insight. You will be challenged by the contents and hopefully expanded and enlarged in your vision to set people free.

The key to breakthrough is living and walking in the Spirit. Jesus cast out devils through the Holy Ghost (see Matt. 12:22-28). There is no other way to success in ministry apart from the Holy Spirit. Carnal and fleshly methods will not do. The flesh profits nothing.

Dependence on the Holy Spirit is a mark of humility and a weapon against the proud spirits we are encountering.

Ana Méndez Ferrell is a pioneer. She has been in the forefront of the spiritual warfare movement for many years. Her understanding did not come from man, but from pressing into the realm of the Spirit. She desires to motivate believers to press into the Spirit themselves. She is reproducing herself through her teaching and preaching. The teaching of this book is a part of her calling and mandate. You will receive an impartation through reading this book.

This book is not an echo of other books. God is releasing a voice, not an echo. Ana has pressed into a new realm of revelation that will open the way for others to follow. The proof of any revelation is found in the results achieved. Are people being set free? Are miracles being released? God is a God of the miraculous. The Holy Spirit is the author of miracles. Apostolic and prophetic revelation is designed to lead us into supernatural lifestyles with supernatural results.

There are multitudes still in captivity. This includes nations and individuals. Jesus came to destroy the works of the devil. He came to authorize and empower believers to do greater works. Knowledge and revelation empowers us. Ignorance of the spirit realm is one of the major reasons why many Christians are ineffective. We are not to be ignorant of spiritual things (see 1 Cor. 12:1).

There are too many leaders who do not operate in the spirit realm and, therefore, cannot teach others how to do so. There are some who are afraid of the spirit realm and, therefore, discourage others from operating in it. This is unfortunate because it prevents us from moving in true power. There are new voices (not echoes) being heard today that are mobilizing the army of the Lord. There are spiritual generals coming on the scene to lead the army with a clear voice and sound. Ana is one of these voices.

Consider what is in this book, and ask the Lord for understanding. Wisdom is the principle thing (see Prov. 4:7), and we desperately need wisdom to meet the challenges of this generation. We especially need wisdom in the areas of deliverance and spiritual warfare. We cannot be ignorant of satan's devices (see 2 Cor. 2:11). We must allow the Holy

Spirit to be our teacher. The Holy Spirit will lead us and guide us into all truth (see John 16:13).

Truth is what sets us free (see John 8:32). The Holy Spirit is the Spirit of Truth. The truth about the regions of captivity needs to be heard throughout the land. Satan's prisons are being exposed. The captives are being set free. The liberators are coming with the keys. The key of truth will unlock every prison. You are one of the liberators. You are one of the deliverers that God is releasing from Zion (see Obad. 1:21).

Those who have been baptized with the Holy Spirit have been immersed in the Spirit realm. God did not give us the Spirit just to speak in tongues, but to be able to operate in the Spirit realm. This book is a clarion call to all Spirit-filled believers to move out and experience the full benefits of the Holy Spirit. As you hear and obey this call, you will be a formidable weapon against the forces of darkness. I encourage you to read, study, and be stirred by the revelation in this book.

Finally, don't be satisfied with milk, but grow into maturity and eat the meat of the word. Meat belongs to them who are of full age. (See Hebrews 5:13-14.)

I believe that apostolic and prophetic revelation will bring us into maturity. It is time for the Church to become more mature in the vital area of deliverance. It is time to grow up. A mature Church will see great expansion of the Kingdom of God. The growth of the Kingdom will release righteousness, peace, and joy in the Holy Ghost. Shalom.

—Apostle John Eckhardt
President and Founder
IMPACT Network and Crusaders Church
Chicago, Illinois, USA

Introduction

This book is a study of one of the most powerful revelations God has given me.

Delivering captives in the traditional manner requires a lot of time, dedication, and physical and spiritual strength—a price few are willing to pay. The battle can be fierce due to the ruthless manifestations of demons. The reality is that this type of deliverance is often unsuccessful. However, there is an easier, more efficient way to deliver people, and it is the way Jesus did it.

Jesus didn't come to earth simply to save us and to die for our sins, but also to give us freedom in every area of our lives. He conquered the devil's empire and *set the captives free*. This goes beyond casting out demons of the occult, drugs, alcohol, and more. Captivity plays a role in the lives of all mankind.

> *The Spirit of the Sovereign Lord is on Me, because the Lord has anointed Me to preach good news to the poor. He has sent Me to bind up the brokenhearted, to proclaim freedom for the captives and release from darkness for the prisoners, to proclaim the year of the Lord's favor and the day of vengeance of our God, to comfort all who mourn, and provide for those who grieve in Zion—to bestow on*

them a crown of beauty instead of ashes, the oil of glad-
ness instead of mourning, and a garment of praise instead
of a spirit of despair. They will be called oaks of righteous-
ness, a planting of the Lord for the display of His splendor
(Isaiah 61:1-3).

Jesus never went to a physical prison to set prisoners free when He was on earth. However, He proclaimed in the synagogue of Nazareth:

Today this scripture is fulfilled in your hearing (Luke 4:21b).

Jesus released many captives from their spiritual prisons through the Holy Spirit. He did it by seeing and hearing what the Father did, through understanding the spiritual world. The Lord desires to empower us with the fullness of the knowledge of His Kingdom.

Freedom from captivity was one of the most important parts of Jesus' suffering and victory through His death and resurrection. Jesus descended to the lowest parts of the earth to take our captivity away from the devil. This freedom is available to all human beings, from the most downtrodden to the most successful. Yet, somehow, parts of our souls are instead held prisoner through sin, sickness, fear, or pain.

Since the children have flesh and blood, He too shared in their
humanity so that by His death He might destroy him who
holds the power of death—that is, the devil—and free those
who all their lives were held in slavery by their fear of death
(Hebrews 2:14-15).

This passage not only refers to the fear of dying, but of everything that pertains to the kingdom of death: poverty, scarcity, sickness, insecurity, sudden tragedy. All of these things control and dominate the majority of human beings, including the Church.

In our days, understanding captivity is of the utmost importance since, many times, receiving and developing our spiritual gifts depends on this knowledge.

> *Therefore He says: "When He ascended on high, He led captivity captive, and gave gifts to men." (Now this, "He ascended"—what does it mean but that He also first descended into the lower parts of the earth? He who descended is also the One who ascended far above all the heavens, that He might fill all things.) And He Himself gave some to be apostles, some prophets, some evangelists, and some pastors and teachers, for the equipping of the saints for the work of ministry, for the edifying of the body of Christ, till we all come to the unity of the faith and of the knowledge of the Son of God, to a perfect man, to the measure of the stature of the fullness of Christ..."* (Ephesians 4:8-13 NKJV).

Jesus dealt with captivity first, then He gave gifts to men so they could develop the Church. This sequence is very important if the Church is to reach its fullness.

The Body of Christ is full of sickness, division, fear, financial scarcity, grave character flaws, lack of understanding, and in many cases lack of vision. These are all symptoms we must consider in order to realize that there may be some things we do not fully understand yet. This breach in our understanding is one of the main reasons why Jesus came to earth: *to take our captivity captive.*

This is a book of deep deliverance and prophetic revelation. Its primary purpose is to advance the Body of Christ to the stature of the "perfect man" (see Eph. 4:13), with apostolic authority.

Every person who has suffered an emotional blow or trauma or has experienced the pain of a broken heart is almost certainly being held captive in some area of life. Anyone who comes from a broken home or from a heritage of occult or blood shedding is in a similar situation. That part of your life where you feel that you do not live in victory or where there is a blockage you can't seem to get around, has to do with captivity.

Once you understand this subject, you will find the answers to the most complicated dilemmas of your inner being. It will help you to recognize the place where you are still held captive (if, in fact, you are) and it will set you free so that you can help others.

It is our work as children of God, to take the Gospel of the glory of Jesus Christ and the Kingdom of God to every creature, so they can be set free and translated from the kingdom of darkness into His wonderful light (see Col. 1:13).

> *Is not this the kind of fasting I have chosen: to loose the chains of injustice and untie the cords of the yoke, to set the oppressed free and break every yoke?* (Isaiah 58:6)

Section One

Regions of Captivity

Chapter 1

The Era
of New Revelations

THIS is a time when God is pouring out treasures of wisdom. The apostolic and prophetic era in which we are living is bringing us new dimensions of Jesus' light. The Scriptures are being understood with far greater clarity. There is an unprecedented revelation of the power and manifestation of the Kingdom of God.

God is raising a spiritual edifice made of people who understand the spiritual arena and operate in the fullness of the Holy Spirit.

The level of revelation depends on the level of love and commitment we have to witness God's work manifested on the earth. We must also understand the pain God suffers as He watches the world being dragged to hell. Several times, He has permitted me to experience His pain so that I might become aware of His burning desire to set souls free.

I WAS IN HELL

Human suffering is something that has marked my life. I have been through very difficult situations. I suffered several years of both verbal and physical abuse that progressed as far as attempted murder by means of strangulation. This occurred at the beginning of my adult life. During this brutal attack, I was dead for several minutes.

At that time, I had not yet received salvation through Jesus, so my soul descended to hell. As I was being strangled, I was surrounded by dark shadows that came for me. I was terrified. I fought for life with all my might, but my efforts were useless.

Little by little, my body surrendered until everything stopped. The pain stopped and I no longer felt the suffocation. My soul descended into a black tunnel, as though sinking into a deep abyss. I heard voices crying in deep suffering.

Slowly, hundreds of beings whose flesh was eaten away approached me. Their bony hands touched me and tried to cover me. Others pulled me from side to side. The horror was indescribable. I screamed, but my voice was lost in the void. There was light in the background, but it was not part of where I was, nor was there access to it. Darkness was all around me. I felt as though all hope had been lost and was now gone forever. My soul shuddered with oppression as I fell into the deep abyss.

It was then that the miraculous hand of God brought me back. Today, I know it was the grace and favor of Jesus that never left me. That experience drives me to fight for lost souls at any cost.

Unfortunately, it took six more years before I met the power of God and His redeeming grace. The trauma of my years of violence and fear led to great emotional instability. I spent two years in therapy with a psychiatrist. During that time and due to my condition, my two children, aged two and three, were taken from me. The pain tore me apart. My soul sank into pits of desperation and agony. The loss of my children stripped me of my desire to live.

It was this desperate condition that led me into the New Age and the occult. As it often does, pain clutched me in its claws. I was easy prey; through continued lies and deceit, my soul was further torn to shreds.

I was diagnosed as a chronic schizophrenic. Tormented by circumstances and spirits of self-destruction, I lost the ability to think coherently.

I tried to commit suicide and was confined to a psychiatric hospital. It was there that the grace and mercy of God reached me and changed my life completely. (You can read my testimony in my book *High Level Warfare*.)

The pain I suffered gave me sensitivity and compassion for the victims of fear, desperation, and sickness. Having been there myself, I understand that they are trapped and tormented in the shifting sands of the soul, unable to get their footing or find a way out.

I hate every form of pain and fear, as they are weapons the devil uses to hurt people. These are the instruments of the empire of darkness to control and subjugate trapped humanity.

Living through years of torment and depression filled me with a holy rage against satan and his destructive work. Setting souls free through the power of Jesus my Redeemer is one of the most important missions in my life. From the time I accepted the Lord as Savior, I made it my goal to be satan's number one enemy for as long as God would give me life.

This call manifested itself the day of my salvation. The first thing that came to my reborn spirit involved how to set the other people in the psychiatric hospital free as well. I knew one thing instantly: if I was there because I had been possessed by demons, then they had the same problem. And, if I was delivered by the power of Jesus of Nazareth, surely they could be, too.

The next day when the pastor came to visit me, the first thing I said was, "How can we set the captives free? They are prisoners just like I was."

Since he was not a scholar of deliverance and this was not a popular teaching in those days in the days when this kind of revelation went largely unnoticed, he replied: "The Bible says that *'these signs will follow those who believe: In My name they will cast out demons; they will speak with new tongues...'"* (Mark 16:17 NKJV).

He went on to ask, "Do you believe?"

With firm conviction, we left my hospital room to set the demented free, one by one. Fifteen days later, 80 percent of the sick had been delivered and healed. To God be the glory!

Later, I began to study in the theological institute that belonged to Pastor Christian Gomez's church. I devoured every book on deliverance that I came across. I understood that this was the beginning of a victorious life in Jesus. Every believer had to be set free in order for the life of the Lord to shine from within, unhindered by blockages.

When the Lord called me to establish my first church, traditional deliverance was a fundamental part of our function. In the majority of cases, we had magnificent results. In others, we were not as successful as we wanted to be. It was as though a piece of the puzzle was missing and it prevented us from having total victory.

Today, after much growth and increased understanding of the spiritual world, I realize how God helped us in our weakness and in the elementary knowledge we had at that time.

THINGS THAT NO MAN HAS CONCEIVED

But as it is written: "Eye has not seen, nor ear heard, nor have entered into the heart of man the things which God has prepared for those who love Him" (1 Corinthians 2:9 NKJV).

In the beginning of the 1980s, the Lord released a wave that was the dawn of the prophetic movement. There was not as much revelation at that time; yet, the simple, passionate love for seeing souls set free allowed God to reveal more truth. As a result, we came to understand the circumstances that give demons the legal right to torment people.

God in His grace supplies all of our lack, but He desires to fill us with wisdom and knowledge. His wish is for us to be mature children with spiritual intelligence.

For this reason, since the day we heard about you, we have not stopped praying for you and asking God to fill you with the knowledge of His will through all spiritual wisdom and understanding (Colossians 1:9).

God desires to reveal to us the deep things of His Kingdom. The light and understanding of the mysteries of the Most High are revealed to us in the measure that we walk in love:

My purpose is that they may be encouraged in heart and united in love, so that they may have the full riches of complete understanding, in order that they may know the mystery of God, namely, Christ, in whom are hidden all the treasures of wisdom and knowledge (Colossians 2:2-3).

The Lord has things for us that have not yet been revealed to other generations. God makes the Church grow from glory to glory and from light to light. The things preached from pulpits today would never have been digested 100 years ago.

The great evangelist Charles Finney changed history during his lifetime. Some time ago I heard a story from someone whose ancestors knew him personally. Before he died, he told me, he burned his personal book of revelations saying, "They are not ready for this," and he destroyed a document that today would be of great inspiration. If this is true, it is indeed a great loss.

Jesus said: *"I have much more to say to you, more than you can now bear"* (John 16:12).

There are things we cannot handle because of our immaturity, our hardness of heart, or our religiosity. Jesus knows which revelations we may or may not be able to understand.

When Jesus ascended into Heaven, He could not tell His disciples all that He would have liked to share. However, He gave the promise of the

Holy Spirit to teach us all things and to help us understand the things Jesus said.

This means that the Spirit brings different depths of teaching, in accordance with the level of our spiritual growth. A person who aspires to great spiritual wisdom and intelligence must spend more time with Him than others. This individual must love God and others and seek answers from the Holy Spirit. Then the things that *"eye has not seen, nor ear heard, nor have entered into the heart of man"* (1 Cor. 2:9 NKJV) will be revealed.

Sometimes I meet people who ask, "Where did you get that? We never heard that before!" Well, God says that there are things that have *never* entered the heart of man, yet He wants to reveal them to us. They are biblical. They have always been in the Scriptures, but they have been closed and veiled so others don't see them.

> He said, *"The knowledge of the secrets of the kingdom of God has been given to you, but to others I speak in parables, so that, 'though seeing, they may not see; though hearing, they may not understand'"* (Luke 8:10).

We have entered a prophetic era and must understand these things. God is empowering this generation with more understanding than those of the past. The same way that science and technology advance, the Word of God is also being revealed in a higher way, to advance the Kingdom of God more effectively.

As we spend our time fighting over words and letting "small foxes" (see Song of Sol. 2:15) rob God's work, millions of people will remain in pain and perdition. They are all waiting for our spiritual growth so they can see the glorious manifestation of the sons and daughters of God.

This is a book that will take you to a different, deeper understanding of the spiritual world—both the realms of God and the world of darkness.

It is my prayer to raise a generation of people who can set the captives free with less effort and greater effectiveness than ever before.

Chapter 2

At Death's Door

For our light and momentary troubles are achieving for us an eternal glory that far outweighs them all. So we fix our eyes not on what is seen, but on what is unseen. For what is seen is temporary, but what is unseen is eternal (2 Corinthians 4:17-18).

It was December 1997. I was about to attend a deliverance training our church had prepared in a hotel outside Mexico City. That night, the spiritual warfare team went to see a movie about military training titled *G.I. Jane.* It had been recommended to me as an example of the tenacity and bravery a woman needed to become an Army Special Forces commando.

There is a moment in the movie in which the commander of the training, who hates G.I. Jane, punches her in the face so hard that the audience cringes. She falls to the floor, almost knocked out. The camera zooms in for a close-up of her face. An invisible force begins to arise from the depths of her heart; you can see it in her facial expression. In the midst of intense pain, this inner strength wells up and she hits the final stroke.

The Holy Spirit fell on me as I watched this scene. I felt Jesus say, *"The final blow is always yours."*

It doesn't matter how great the pain is, the power of God's love will always rise within us to give us the final blow of victory. (For those who have reservations about going to the movies, please set that aside. God can use anything to talk to us: a donkey, a dried fig tree, a movie. We are cautious about what we see. The truth is that God is using some movies to open the eyes of many. To Him and Him alone be the glory.)

Only Jesus knew how this scene would help me to deal with the terrible blow the devil would deliver at the retreat the next day. We had traveled for more than two hours out of the city and had barely gotten settled in order to begin the event, when I received a call that would change the course of my Christian life.

The call was my beloved friend, Cecilia Pezet. Her voice quivered with extreme emotional pain. "I am in the hospital with your sister Mercedes. She is in critical condition. I brought her to be examined. They have just given me her test results. She has three brain tumors and they just took her into surgery."

I froze. Mercedes had been dizzy the previous week. We all thought—even her doctor—that an inner ear problem had made her unsteady.

Please understand what I felt at that moment. Mercedes was my identical twin. We were born from one egg that divided into two. I was not born alone, like the majority of people. I was born with my twin. God joined us from the womb with a very special bond. For 42 years, we had always been together; even when we were separated by distance, in soul we remained inseparable.

Perhaps only those who are twins can understand what happened to me when Cecilia called. It was evident to me that my sister's life was in danger, and I was convinced in my heart that the only thing I could not overcome in life would be to lose her, if she were, in fact, to die.

This news was so sudden and unexpected. I felt the devil's blow so sharply, just as I had seen it in the movie. But I also felt that strength that arose from the depths of my being. It was not the human strength of a soldier, but the very power of Jesus that conquered satan in hell. In that very moment, in the midst of unspeakable pain, I knew that God would permit me to have the final blow.

VICTORY IN ACTION

A torturous path began with Mercedes' diagnosis. It lasted four years, during which time my sister died six times, and six times, was raised by God from the dead. At the end of those four years, there came a point at which God said that it was time for her to go.

Yet those years, so full of pain, were also filled with glory. They were perhaps the best years of Mercedes' ministry. She ministered to many people from her wheelchair. She called it her "Chariot of Fire." From that chair, she had the most marvelous experiences with God. She ministered to even the strongest among us. She also encouraged others who were in wheelchairs. She taught them to look at the invisible side of things, where God manifests Himself.

During that difficult time, Mercedes organized the entire nation in "Glory Marches" that made history in Mexico. Hundreds of thousands of people praised God in the streets and in the central plaza of the capital. The marches continued even after her death. But we will always remember Mercedes in her wheelchair, marching and praising God.

For me, those years were truly a kind of "Spirit University." Even the revelation contained in this book is the result of fighting for my sister's life. I learned that when you truly love, the fight will always lead to victory. I also learned this important truth: *Defeat dwells in passivity. Even when hope and faith are present, inaction will result in a battle lost.* This revelation dispels the deception that God will do everything simply because we raise a prayer to Heaven.

We are closest to the most powerful manifestations of God when we are in the most difficult circumstances, those in which it seems there is no way out. We must wait for His voice and hear His instructions.

God always gives us the answer. The tough times we go through bring a greater level of authority from God, if we are positioned for the victory.

During the Exodus, God put Moses and the Israelites in Pi Hahiroth, a narrow place with no way of escape. Pharaoh thought the people of Israel were surrounded; he was confident the desert had closed them in. (see Exodus 14:1-3.)

However, Moses trusted in Jehovah. Even so, not everything would happen from a passive position.

> *Moses answered the people, "Do not be afraid. Stand firm and you will see the deliverance the Lord will bring you today. The Egyptians you see today you will never see again. The Lord will fight for you; you need only to be still." Then the Lord said to Moses, "Why are you crying out to Me? Tell the Israelites to move on. Raise your staff and stretch out your hand over the sea to divide the water so that the Israelites can go through the sea on dry ground"* (Exodus 14:13-16).

God instructed Moses and the Israelites to *take action.* The same is true in our personal lives—and I know one thing for sure: nobody will fight harder for our loved ones than we will with the power of God.

During one of her surgeries, Mercedes had complications and contracted pneumonia. She had few defenses left and the cold of the operating room caused the infection. Due to her weakened condition, phlegm turned into a hard mass in her lungs. There was no way to get it out. Finally, the doctor said she would die. We had already done everything we knew to do in the areas of spiritual warfare and divine healing, but nothing worked. We were hours away from losing Mercedes.

In my desperation, I called what was then the World Prayer Center, where I worked with C. Peter Wagner on warfare initiatives. Prophet Chuck Pierce answered the phone and made a statement that would change everything. "Ana," he said, "get in deep communion with God. He is about to give you the key that will not only save Mercedes' life, but He will teach you to fight against dominions and principalities at a higher level."

I received the prophetic word and began to seek God with all my heart. The Lord then spoke in my ear the following passage from the Book of Job:

> *Have the gates of death been revealed to you? Or have you seen the doors of the shadow of death? Have you comprehended the breadth of the earth? Tell Me, if you know all this. Where is the way to the dwelling of light? And darkness, where is its place, that you may take it to its territory, that you may know the paths to its home?* (Job 38:17-20 NKJV)

After reading it, I was perplexed because I really didn't understand what God wanted to tell me. The answer to those questions was, of course, "No, I do not know the answers to any of these questions."

Confused, I asked Him what it was that He wanted to teach me. Then He said, "Mercedes is trapped in the gate of the shadow of death. You must go for her and bring her back."

When I heard this, I was speechless. I knew it was the Father speaking to me, but I didn't know what to do with His instructions. "The shadow of death, Lord?" I asked, "Am I going to die?" He didn't answer me.

I told Apostle Rony Chaves, the person in authority over me, what I had heard. I told him that I didn't have any right to continue teaching about the love of God if I didn't do everything in my power for the person I loved the most. I asked for his blessing and for him to pray for me the next day at 7:00 A.M. At that time, I would go to God to seek that place, and if I didn't return, I wanted Rony to know that I had died trying. I spoke with my intercessors and asked our church to pray for me.

At 7:00 A.M., I was in communion with the Spirit. On one hand, I was nervous; on the other, I was expectant. I had full confidence in God and

I had determined to do whatever was necessary, even put my own life on the line, to save my sister.

Then the weight of His glory began to come upon me.

It was like a heavenly invasion that entered the room. Two angels appeared in front of me. Their clothing was glowing and there was tremendous strength in their facial expressions. One of them had a chain with golden keys on it. He was the leader and with a firm, sweet voice, he said, "Follow us!"

I got up from the bed in my spiritual body and followed them. It was as though I were entering a heavenly vision. We began to walk on the city streets until we arrived at a drain in the road. One of the angels opened the drain and we descended into enormous pipes. (This was interesting, since my sister had dedicated herself to rescuing street children who lived in the sewers.)

We walked a long time through the damp, dark drainage pipes. The only light emanated from the clothing of my companions. Then we arrived at a hole in the ground. It seemed like an old pipe, worn and moldy, about two meters wide. It smelled like death and decay. Nailed to the wall of this pit was an iron ladder that descended to a deeper place.

It was a dark, cold tunnel. All along the tunnel were vertical beds of sick people with IVs and catheters. I began to look for Mercedes, hoping to see her somewhere. The angel said we had not yet arrived where she was. We walked among the patients, who moaned continually. Some cried in such pain that it made my soul shudder.

My heart wanted to help them in some way, but I didn't know where we were or how to help. I focused on obeying the directions of the angel with total submission.

We opened a second hole that was extremely narrow and oppressive. One of my guides jumped weightlessly through the opening. I followed him, and behind us came the second messenger. It felt like I was sinking into an abyss of water, with my own weight pulling me to the bottom.

Mercedes in the Prison of The Shadow of Death.

We arrived at a deep place that was very cold. A long corridor extended in front of us, with cells on both sides. It was like an old medieval dungeon. There were about ten prisoners in each cell. In the second cell, I saw Mercedes. Everyone there had on gray clothing, but she was dressed in white and was curled up on a stone bed in the back of the cell.

Suddenly, my mouth opened and I shouted loudly, "Mercedes, come forth!"

In that moment, I understood what Jesus did when he called Lazarus from the grave. He was not only calling him out of the physical tomb, but he was taking him from the depths of Sheol.

The angel interrupted me and said that Mercedes could not leave there by herself. I needed to go in there and get her. He took a beautiful key that he had with him and opened the door. I went to where she was and carried her over my shoulder. She didn't weigh anything. I took her out of there and the angel told me to put her on the floor. He told me to impart the power of the resurrection, lying on top of her like Elisha had done (see 2 Kings 4:34). I did it and she became full of life and stood up beside us.

The angel closed the cell and we went back the same way we had come. A little later, Mercedes, the angels, and I found ourselves back in my bedroom. Then the angel told me it was necessary to reunite my sister's soul with the rest of her soul in the hospital.

I came back from the spiritual arena and got into my car. I still felt the presence of the angels and Mercedes. All three of them got into the car with me. We arrived at the hospital and the fragmented part of Mercedes' soul that had been captive, reintegrated with her body.

Immediately, the power of resurrection gave my sister new strength; she coughed up the phlegm ball and became totally healed. The next day, she left the hospital.

It took me days to assimilate the experience. It was like the joy a miner feels when he strikes a vein of gold and knows that he has tapped only the tip of the iceberg of incalculable riches.

After this experience, I sought God for more on this subject. I realized that thousands of other people could be trapped someplace. A rain of revelation began to pour over me. The Bible was opened in a new, powerful way, uncovering things that had always been there, but that I had simply never seen before.

The first thing I understood was the way in which the soul operates. The enemy fragments and imprisons our souls. I witnessed the spiritual world and its different regions, the prisons in which souls are kept captive. I also saw the devil's destructive designs. I learned to break through and take the captive souls out through Jesus Christ.

Please allow me to begin laying out this thread of knowledge, one step at a time. It will bring understanding of how we can fall captive *and* how we can be set free.

Chapter 3

Heavenly and Infernal Places

In the spiritual world, there are two kingdoms: the Kingdom of Light and the kingdom of darkness. In the Kingdom of God, or in what is known as Heaven, the Bible mentions several regions that it calls "heavenly places."

> *And God raised us up with Christ and seated us with Him*
> *in the heavenly realms in Christ Jesus* (Ephesians 2:6).

Just as there are heavenly places, there are also places or regions of darkness which we can call *infernal places.* I use the word *infernal* as an adjective commonly used to classify things related to the devil. As we will see, not all of these regions are tied with hell, the final destiny of the lost.

These two large spiritual regions, or kingdoms of light and darkness, continually affect the land of the living. We don't have to be dead for Heaven to manifest itself in our lives; likewise, we need not die for our lives to become a living hell.

The mission of our Lord was to unite Heaven and earth again, in bringing the Kingdom of God. The goal was to cause everything that belongs to the heavenly Kingdom to be established in the natural world:

He made known to us the mystery of His will according to His good pleasure, which He purposed in Christ, to be put into effect when the times will have reached their fulfillment—to bring all things in heaven and on earth together under one head, even Christ (Ephesians 1:9-10).

Jesus fills the earth every day with His mercy and blessings. Heaven intervenes on behalf of the just and the unjust, trying to bring all men closer to the heavenly Father. He manifests God's designs on earth, sends angels to help us, and fights together with us. He is seating us in heavenly places with Him, which means we can be in Heaven and on the earth at the same time.

Jesus lived, immersed in a heavenly reality, just as palpable and visible as the natural world. He came to unite heaven and earth, so we can experience and enjoy the reality of heaven with its blessings while we are on earth.

No one has ascended to heaven but He who came down from heaven, that is, the Son of Man who is in heaven (John 3:13 NKJV).

As the scripture reads, Jesus is at the same time in Heaven and on earth. He speaks about ascending to Heaven as if he has gone up before His final ascension from the Mount of Olives. In this verse he clearly declares that *He is in Heaven.*

By contrast, the mission of the devil, who imitates God, is precisely the opposite—to unite the earth and hell under his kingdom and thereby control, oppress, rob, and kill the whole world.

The workings of hell are clearly visible among the people. It brings death, sickness, destruction, strife, and all kinds of evil to the world.

The cords of the grave coiled around me; the snares of death confronted me (Psalms 18:5).

The Bible also speaks about those who are prisoners of sin.

Snatch others from the fire and save them (Jude 1:23a).

When Jude speaks about snatching someone out of hell, he doesn't refer to people that are dead and condemned, but is speaking about people that are bound by the power of hell, prisoners of sin and horrible circumstances.

It is important to understand that *this is not referring to taking the dead from their eternal dwelling place, but of delivering the living who are trapped in the devil's fire.*

Satan's demons, headquarters, lines of communication, and so forth are all well established on the earth. Unbelievers often say hell is here, on this plane. Although hell is real and is the place of eternal perdition, they can feel its effects on the earth. That is why they are confused about its eternal implications.

DESIGNS IN THE SPIRITUAL WORLD

Both kingdoms function by designs established in the spiritual world and manifested in our lives. God's designs originate in heavenly places and the devil's designs come from infernal places. Understanding the operations of these designs is of the utmost importance in order to understand why certain things happen.

One of the greatest revelations of God for me came while I was praying for a pastor in the hospital. God was talking to me about captivity, and this experience really brought light to the subject.

The pastor's condition was considered terminal, so I got into the Spirit to try to see the spiritual world around him and find how I could help him. Suddenly, it was as if the Lord gave me a vision. I appeared in a place that was one of the regions of darkness. It was a gloomy, cold room and the sick brother was in there, in the same hospital bed in which I had already seen him, with the same tubes attached to his body. It was an exact replica of the visible realm. The place was full of demons speaking over the sick man. He was a holy man, a servant of God who the devil wanted to kill.

I asked the Holy Spirit about the location and He answered: *"In the chambers of the designs of hell. I want you to get closer to listen to what the demons are saying. I want to teach you something."*

I got closer, and I clearly heard them chanting in unison: "Oh, satan, satan, your will be done on earth, as it is in hell."

I was speechless as the Spirit of the Lord explained how the devil has made plans in the kingdom of darkness against all of us and that his servants of the underworld are establishing them upon the earth.

While the majority of Christians never pray to pull God's designs toward themselves, it is certain that the demons continually pray for the devil's plans to prosper.

Likewise, we should pray for God's plans to prosper. The Lord's Prayer is a very powerful diagram to apostolically establish God's designs on the earth. It should not be recited, but understood. It is a divine teaching to establish God's Kingdom and blessings in our lives.

The prayer leads us step by step. One begins by entering into His presence, in deep adoration and exaltation of the heavenly Father. Once there, we pull down, from Heaven to earth, everything He has designed for us.

> *This...is how you should pray: "Our Father in heaven, hallowed be Your name, Your kingdom come, **Your will be done on earth as it is in heaven**"* (Matthew 6:9-10).

The devil is an imitator and knows how to unite the visible with the invisible. He uses the power of curses and witchcraft to establish his designs upon the earth.

Now, returning to the scene where I found myself in that diabolical chamber, I asked the Lord what I should do. He responded saying, *"The*

Chamber of the Designs of Hell

Ananda Lamas Valle
anandalamas@gmail.com

Son of God was manifested to destroy the works of the devil, not only on the face of the earth, but to the depths of hell where they originate. The Word of faith decreed from a spirit united to Jesus does not stop on the surface of the earth. It has power to penetrate the heavens, hell, and the invisible world."

So I declared that Word, with all the power of God, and instantly, the place vanished before my eyes with all the demons. I came back from my vision to the hospital room where the brother was. The atmosphere of death that surrounded him disappeared. His face began to fill with the life of Jesus that lived within him. In a couple of days, he was released from the hospital in perfect health.

The Lord spoke to me clearly about the designs of the devil and backed it up with His Word through Psalm 74, some of which is quoted next.

Many believe and teach in biblical institutes that Psalms is a book of poetry, but King David and the psalmists were not poets, they were prophets. It is clear that, in Psalm 74 Asaph, one of the singers in David's tabernacle, lifted up a prophetic prayer of deep spiritual understanding. These psalms came from Heaven and from the wisdom of God. They were definitely led by the Holy Spirit through the prophetic anointing that moved in that tent of worship.

In Psalm 74, the destruction of God's assembly originates in the place of *"perpetual desolations,"* the devil's strategic planning room. Asaph cries out to God to direct His steps to this infernal place because it is from there that this evil has been produced.

> *O God, why have You cast us off forever? Why does Your anger smoke against the sheep of Your pasture? Remember Your congregation, which You have purchased of old, the tribe of Your inheritance, which You have redeemed— this Mount Zion where You have dwelt. Lift up Your feet to the **perpetual desolations**. The enemy has damaged everything in the sanctuary. Your enemies roar in the*

midst of Your meeting place; they set up their banners for signs. They seem like men who lift up axes among the thick trees. And now they break down its carved work, all at once, with axes and hammers. They have set fire to Your sanctuary; they have defiled the dwelling place of Your name to the ground. They said in their hearts, "Let us destroy them altogether." They have burned up all the meeting places of God in the land (Psalms 74:1-8 NKJV).

I have seen similar things while praying for churches or ministries that were being destroyed by the power of the devil. If we live in ignorance of our enemy's devices, without hitting the bull's eye with our prayers, the devil will attack, kill, and destroy. This is what we see happening in thousands of congregations all over the face of the earth.

One of the ways in which the devil activates his designs is through witchcraft. Allow me to explain how it works. The word *witchcraft* points to something that is crafted, as in an object or a work. It is something done to produce evil in a person, business, or city. For this evil to work, it needs a design concocted under the inspiration of spirits of witchcraft. The sorcerer needs something that represents the person or project to be harmed.

Let's take the well-known example of a voodoo doll with pins sticking out of it. Whatever the witch does on earth, the devil reproduces in hell and vice versa. From hell, the demons keep the design alive so that it manifests in the life of the person. This is a crude copy of a heavenly principle made by God:

I tell you the truth, whatever you bind on earth will be bound in heaven, and whatever you loose on earth will be loosed in heaven. Again, I tell you that if two of you on earth agree about anything you ask for, it will be done for you by My Father in heaven (Matthew 18:18-19).

The devil never invented anything. He steals the principles of God and perverts them to suit his purposes. The power that Jesus gave us to bind and loose is one of the ways God gives us authority to pull His designs down from Heaven to earth.

Once I understand the way the devil operates, I begin to direct my prayers toward the destruction of the works of the devil, to the very places where they originate. When I pray for someone and discover by the Spirit of God the design that is operating in the person's life, I simply pray:

> "The Son of God was manifested to destroy the works of the devil to the very depths of hell. And in this moment, I loose the manifestation of Jesus, the Son of God, tearing to pieces every design of the devil in the kingdom of darkness. Amen."

There are people whom God has trained in the prophetic. They see the structures of darkness and what the devil is doing; but not everyone can. However, every person can decree by faith the principles in this book and God will back them up.

It is written in Heaven that Jesus, the Son of God, destroyed the works of the devil. When your prayer connects with this truth, the power of God is loosed and the works of the devil are undone.

There are people under designs of failure, financial ruin, poverty, debt, divorce, family destruction, sickness, accidents, and many other things. Thousands of people will enter a new level of freedom when we undo those designs that bind them.

First, however, we must dispel a misconception that keeps people from uncovering the enemy's designs. I would like to clarify a verse that some people use for not wanting to understand the depths of hell. We find it in one of the seven letters of Revelation:

But unto you I say, and unto the rest in Thyatira, as many as have not this doctrine, and which have not known the depths of Satan... (Revelation 2:24 KJV).

According to the context of the passage, this verse refers to the doctrine of Jezebel, to spiritual fornication, and to the sacrifices made to idols. The key word here is the verb *to know,* which implies intimate communion.[1] It is not referring to people who simply understand the designs of satan. It refers to the danger of entering into relationship with the devil and participating in the occult that binds the spirit of man with satan, producing the most abominable fornication.

In this book, we are dealing with the work of Christ destroying the power of hell. Jesus Himself descended to the lowest parts of the earth; yet that does not mean that He knew the depths of satan. Dealing with this subject, I consulted several apostles and theologians. Apostle Samuel Arboleda of Peru wrote to me a letter that said to say the following:

> I believe that the gift of prophetic knowledge is given by the Holy Spirit in order to penetrate the kingdom of darkness where God wants to show us key aspects that will set people free. It does not deal with going down to hell for the sake of going there or penetrating it just to penetrate it. The person the Lord chooses to experience it does this type of deliverance under the direction of God, through His Spirit.

> 1. Seeing it, penetrating it, or traveling to the arenas of the kingdom of darkness does not proceed from a specific methodology (such as used by witches or spiritualists), but is a prophetic and apostolic action by the Spirit of God in His servants, who are given the gift of knowledge or revelation of dreams or visions, in order to carry out a deliverance from captivity. Revelation 2:24 warns against the distortion of this powerful weapon. Revelation 2:24 does

not prohibit this prophetic truth because the same Spirit is showing John the captivities into which the false prophets will fall—sickness, great tribulation, and their children will be fatally wounded.

2. The gift of knowledge and revelation of dreams or visions, by the work of the Spirit of God, leads you to know, walk, observe, discern, and receive precise direction from God, allowing you to move with certainty and efficiency. Normally, you are in a certain place, frequently in front of the person needing deliverance and from there you can operate without the need to describe that you are walking through hell. I believe that the practical explanation of what to do and how to apply deliverance from the regions of captivity is very clearly laid out in your book.[2]

Chapter 7 of this book covers some of the deliverance concepts to which Apostle Arboleda refers. We will get to those soon, but first—more insight on the nature of captivity and the hindrances to breakthrough.

ENDNOTES

1. *Biblesoft's New Exhaustive Strong's Numbers and Concordance with Expanded Greek-Hebrew Dictionary.* CD-ROM. Biblesoft, Inc. and International Bible Translators, Inc. s.v. "ginosko" (NT 1097).

2. Apóstol Samuel Arboleda Lima Perú, www.impactperu.org.

Chapter 4

Captivity and the Cities in Ruin

The goal of the devil's empire is to take prisoners, to subjugate them, to oppress them, to rob them of every gift of God and, finally, to destroy them. Satan uses slavery to cut the wings of the spirit with which we soar to the heights of God.

The devil governs through a spiritual city called Babylon, which opposes the heavenly city, the New Jerusalem. Babylon is the devil's general headquarters; several spiritual regions arrayed under Babylon combine with it to compose his kingdom of terror and death.

> *The woman you saw is the great city that rules over the kings of the earth* (Revelation 17:18).

JESUS CAME TO SET THE CAPTIVES FREE

Jesus not only came to save us from sin, but also to rescue us from our captivity and from all that implies the kingdom of darkness: sickness, death, brokenness, anguish, poverty, etc.

> *The Spirit of the Lord God is upon Me, because the Lord has anointed Me to preach good tidings to the poor; He has sent Me to heal the brokenhearted, **to proclaim***

liberty to the captives, and the opening of the prison to those who are bound... (Isaiah 61:1 NKJV).

The captivities and prisons to which this passage refers are not physical, but spiritual. God does not set criminals free who have been sentenced to jail. The Kingdom of God respects order and a nation's criminal justice system and acknowledges the right exercised by the law to incarcerate those who do evil. Still, His anointing can set free those who are innocent prisoners, as in the cases of Peter (see Acts 12:5-10) and Paul and Silas (see Acts 16:22-26).

The reality is that the kingdom of darkness is formed of thousands and millions of prisons, where satan holds the human race captive.

*I, the Lord, have called You in righteousness; I will take hold of Your hand. I will keep You and will make You to be a covenant for the people and a light for the Gentiles, to open eyes that are blind, **to free captives from prison and to release from the dungeon those who sit in darkness** (Isaiah 42:6-7).*

and free those who all their lives were held in slavery by their fear of death (Hebrews 2:15).

The problem is in thinking that captivity is only for persons who have "social problems." Drug addicts, prostitutes, and alcoholics are not the only ones occupying satan's prison chambers.

We also err by assuming that, once satan's captives give up their vices, they leave their prisons and are free from slavery. In reality, the matter is much more complex than that; the end of troubling behavior does not necessarily indicate the end of captivity.

Again, these issues are not restricted to certain groups of people; instead they concern us all. The truth is that any person can be captive—

Christians included. The Bible shows us how even God's prophets, such as King David, lived as captives in spiritual prisons.

> *Bring my soul out of prison, that I may praise Your name; the righteous shall surround me, for You shall deal bountifully with me* (Psalms 142:7 NKJV).

King David was never in a physical prison. However, the man whose son would build the most extraordinary temple of worship ever constructed told God he couldn't worship because his soul was in prison.

This is the reality of millions of people who are unable to worship or function in other areas of their lives. There are people who are happy during the Sunday morning service, yet are defeated by sadness, rage, and anguish that same afternoon.

Millions of Christians cannot find their breakthrough when it comes to the areas of health, character, and finances. One day they are at their peak; the next day they are in the valley. This is so because Jesus' victory over captivity is almost an unknown subject in the Church.

> *Hear and pay attention, do not be arrogant, for the Lord has spoken. Give glory to the Lord your God...**before your feet stumble on the darkening hills**. You hope for light, but He will turn it to **thick darkness** and change it to **deep gloom**. But if you do not listen, I will weep in secret because of your pride; my eyes will weep bitterly, overflowing with tears, because **the Lord's flock will be taken captive*** (Jeremiah 13:15-17).

God is reforming all things and taking His pioneers, apostles, and prophets from revelation to revelation. This is one of those revelations. So, let's understand how a faithful Christian, who loves God, can experience a prison of the soul from which he can find no escape.

THE FRAGMENT OF THE SOUL

The soul and spirit are ultimately connected and made of a substance that can be fragmented. Our souls contain the information defining who we are as spiritual beings.

There is a parallel in the physical realm: Inside the nucleus of our cells is found a substance called DNA, which is a chain of amino acids. It works like a file in which all the genetic information about the physical being is found. If we had the technology to accomplish it, an entire body could be reproduced from a single cell.

Likewise, a single fragment of the soul is all that is needed to capture us spiritually. The devil does not need to possess the entire soul to take a prisoner in the spiritual sphere. He only needs a fragment to establish in it a region of his kingdom and from there afflict it.

In order for this to happen, the devil must shatter the soul through circumstances, causing deep fear, trauma, or acute pain. In addition, he can divide the soul through participation in the occult and sin. Figure 1 illustrates the condition of such a soul; instead of picturing wholeness, the shattered soul consists of many jagged and pierced pieces.

In biblical symbolism, when the Lord talks about Judah, it often has to do with the human soul, whereas when Jerusalem is talked about, it often has to do with the human spirit. The people of Israel in the Old Testament serve as a symbol of the spiritual condition of the Church. Taking this into account, let's look at the devil's devices to fragment souls in the Scriptures.

> *Let us go against Judah and harass and terrify it; and let us cleave it a sunder [each of us taking a portion], and set a [vassal] king in the midst of it, namely the son of Tabeal* (Isaiah 7:6 AMP).[1]

All of us have been victims at some time or other of terrifying or painful situations. These are moments in which something breaks in the

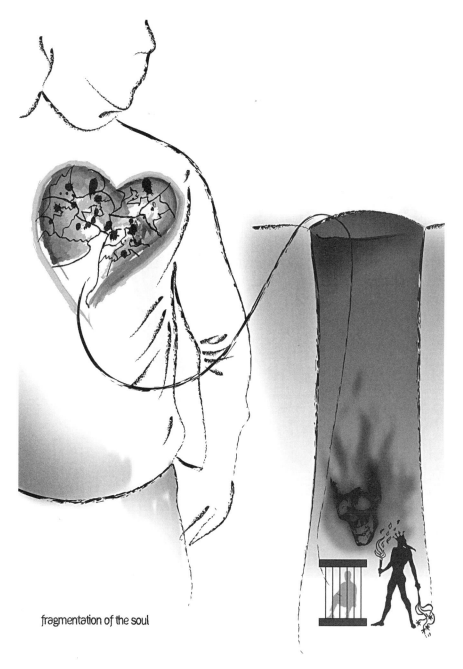

fragmentation of the soul

Figure 1

Ananda Lamas Valle
anandalamas@gmail.com

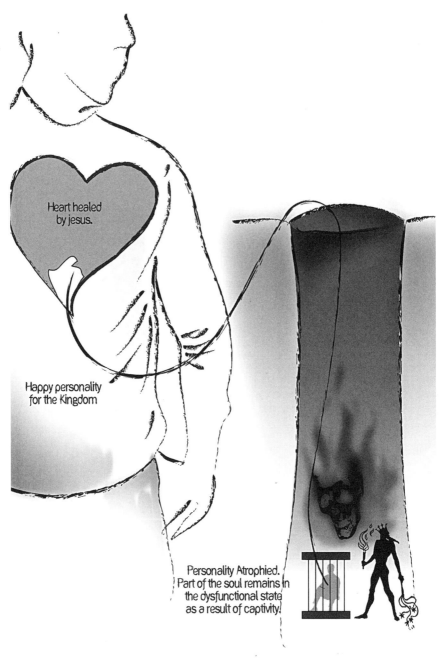

Heart healed
by jesus.

Happy personality
for the Kingdom

Personality Atrophied.
Part of the soul remains in
the dysfunctional state
as a result of captivity.

Figure 2

Ananda Lamas Valle
anandalamas@gmail.com

depths of our being. Expressions such as, "I'm broken up," or, "They broke my heart," reflect the injuries inflicted upon the soul during fragmentation. The devil takes advantage of moments of great suffering to capture a piece of us and take us as prisoners in his kingdom—even when most of the soul has been healed through Christ.

Once the soul has been broken, satan makes us "good for nothing" in that area of our lives, or in *every* area in some cases.[2]

King David clearly understood that he had a spiritual enemy who stalked his soul in order to destroy it.

> *For without cause they hid for me their net; a pit of destruction without cause they dug for my life* [my soul]....*Lord, how long will You look on [without action]? Rescue my life* [my soul] *from their destructions, my dear and only life from the lions!* (Psalms 35:7,17 AMP)

In these Scriptures, the enemies of David are not only physical, but also spiritual. To God, the soul is like a city that can be destroyed. If this happens, it must be rebuilt in order to function properly. (Please note that, although many English renderings of Psalms 35:17 include the phrase *"Rescue my life,"* other translations, such as the King James Version, render the same phrase as *"Rescue my soul."*)

> *But you are a chosen people, a royal priesthood, a holy nation* [city], *a people belonging to God, that you may declare the praises of Him who called you out of darkness into His wonderful light* (1 Peter 2:9).

When the devil breaks our soul, it is as if our inner city becomes desolate and in ruins. Therefore, when we first come to Jesus, we need to begin a process of restoration and deliverance. This is a rebuilding of the old ruins. We all need to be rebuilt so that the temple of God can be constructed within us. We need the designs of the devil to be destroyed in our lives so we can be set totally free.

This is what the Lord says—your Redeemer, who formed you in the womb: I am the Lord, who has made all things, who alone stretched out the heavens, who spread out the earth by Myself, who foils the signs of false prophets and makes fools of diviners, who overthrows the learning of the wise and turns it into nonsense, who carries out the words of His servants and fulfills the predictions of His messengers, who says of Jerusalem, "It shall be inhabited," of the towns of Judah, "They shall be built," and of their ruins, "I will restore them" (Isaiah 44:24-26).

It is the work of Jesus to completely destroy the work of the devil through the anointing of the Holy Spirit. This is a process that does not end with the announcement and acceptance of the Good News of the Gospel.

*The Spirit of the Sovereign Lord is on Me, because the Lord has anointed Me to preach good news to **the poor**. He has sent Me to bind up **the brokenhearted**, to proclaim freedom for the captives and release from darkness for **the prisoners**, to proclaim the year of the Lord's favor and the day of vengeance of our God, to comfort all who mourn, and provide for **those who grieve** in Zion—to bestow on them a crown of beauty instead of ashes, the oil of gladness instead of mourning, and a garment of praise instead of a spirit of despair. They will be called oaks of righteousness, a planting of the Lord for the display of His splendor. **They will rebuild the ancient ruins** and restore the places long devastated; **they will renew the ruined cities** that have been devastated for generations* (Isaiah 61:1-4).

I have set the key words in bold in this passage because I want you to appreciate the liberating work of the Lord.

God wants to raise us up as kings and priests for God the Father. The kings of the Kingdom of God have shining cities. There is no king without a territory, without abundant riches, or without authority. Everything the king says is law. But as long as Tabeal governs, a part of each of our souls will be useless. We will not be in control of our lives; we will live with confusion, terror, sickness, and the feeling that we are powerless to overcome.

> And you will be called priests of the Lord, you will be named ministers of our God. **You will feed on the wealth of nations, and in their riches you will boast.** Instead of their shame My people will receive a double portion, and instead of disgrace they will rejoice in their inheritance; and so **they will inherit a double portion in their land, and everlasting joy will be theirs** (Isaiah 61:6-7).

The apostolic anointing is what opens our understanding, enabling us to take authority—as the kings we are in Christ—over the gates of hell.

As Jesus told Peter, *"The gates of hell will not prevail against the Church"* (see Matt. 16:18). Behind those gates are captive kings, sons of God, who are unsuccessful at being who they are meant to be because the devil has rendered them useless. Spiritual and material treasures are also being held back from those kings. But God is raising a generation of men and women with understanding, with the anointing of Cyrus, King of Persia, to restore and raise kings and set the prisoners free.

> Thus says the Lord to His anointed, to Cyrus, whose right hand I have held—to subdue nations before him and loose the armor of kings, to open before him the double doors, so that the gates will not be shut: "I will go before you and make the crooked places straight; I will break in pieces the gates of bronze and cut the bars of iron. I will give you the treasures of darkness and hidden riches of secret places,

*that you may know that I, the Lord, who call you by your
name, am the God of Israel"* (Isaiah 45:1-3 NKJV).

The soul that has been broken and locked up in prison is going to be tormented by everything that it sees, feels, and hears around it in the spiritual region of its captivity. It is trapped behind iron gates in regions of evil in the kingdom of darkness.

In the story I told about my sister who was imprisoned in the region called "the gate of the shadow of death," we saw the place that affected her. This prison affected her life; little by little, her soul was impregnated with the death-ridden atmosphere that surrounded her. Inevitably, if she had not been rescued, death would have sucked the life out of her and killed her.

My sister was a precious servant of the Lord whose final destiny was Heaven, but who was not destined by God to die ahead of time. The gates of hell could not prevail because Christ gave us the victory.

Captivities are strictly spiritual places controlled by the hosts of satan. Willpower is not enough to free souls from these places; we need God's authority to move against the forces of darkness.

There are many reasons why a soul can be captive. The fire of hell traps both the just and the unjust. Anyone can be exposed to traumas, spells, and spiritual traps. For example, when a patient is under anesthesia or when a soul becomes heartbroken while visiting a cemetery, the person enters the regions of death. These regions can also be entered via the emotion of fear or by doing spiritual warfare with insufficient understanding.

Another cause of exposure is found in bringing the Gospel to enemy-controlled territories without the laying of appropriate spiritual groundwork. Some are born into captivity because of a parent's imprisonment. This is a form of generational captivity that relates to our discussion of broken cities as symbols of the soul.

*They will rebuild the ancient ruins and restore the places long devastated; they will renew **the ruined cities that have been devastated for generations*** (Isaiah 61:4).

This is the case in children who are born with autism and locked inside themselves in a world assigned to them in spiritual regions. There are other forms of captivity that occur in a variety of ways. Babies can become trapped when parents attempt abortion. Even the fetus who suffers the intense pain of a tormented mother while in the womb can be held captive. Many times these souls don't want to be born because they are already trapped in regions of death.

Phobias such as claustrophobia, agoraphobia, the fear of heights, the fear of the dark, or anything else that scares us, have to do with captivity of the soul.

During my childhood, I was traumatized while playing with my brothers and sisters. They caught an enormous moth and put it inside the back of my blouse. I screamed in terror, feeling the animal trapped inside my clothing, but unable to get out. Instead of helping me, my siblings laughed at me. This produced a fear of all butterflies and moths. Even as an adult, I would lose my composure at the sight of one.

When I became a Christian, I tried several times to be set free from this form of panic; but no matter what anyone did, I remained trapped by the phobia. It wasn't until I discovered the principles I am sharing with you that I was able to be set free.

As I said before, the soul sees, feels, and hears everything that surrounds it in the place where it is imprisoned. The fragment of my soul shattered after the incident with the moth was held captive in a dark cell full of black butterflies that flew around me chaotically and beat their wings against my face and body. In that place, the horror that I experienced as a child perpetuated itself. As a consequence, whenever I physically saw one of these creatures, my conscious being would connect with my imprisoned soul. The terror I was living in that cell would then flood me and I would lose control.

This was not the only captivity I suffered. My soul was broken many times by the enemy. One by one, I had to go to each prison to retrieve my soul. Today, I am a whole person, full of bravery and fullness in every area of my life. The devil can no longer frighten me. Glory to God!

The imprisoned soul of a child of God can never totally develop. By the grace of God, it will reach a certain level, but it will never go beyond that point. Many servants of God have died before their time. Many live in slavery to medicines or suffer destruction without reason. Others live from surgery to surgery, in lack and need. It doesn't have to be this way. Jesus already took captivity captive. Now it is our turn to be set free.

So, let's uncover many of those places that make up the kingdom of darkness.

ENDNOTES

1. It is interesting that once the soul has been broken, the devil allows the son of Tabeal to reign over it. There is not much we know from the Bible about this king except from the meaning of his name. In Aramaic, *Tabeal* means "good for nothing." From NAS Hebrew concordance.

2. 2870a. lAaVbDfTabeal [370b]; from 2895 and 408; "good for nothing," Aramaic.

Chapter 5

Spiritual Realms Revealed

There are both heavenly places and regions of darkness, as mentioned previously. They are spiritual places because they are not limited by time or space as we know it on earth.

The spiritual places have nothing to do with our geography on earth. They belong to a different dimension than ours; nevertheless, they can affect or be over a physical region. Such is the case of Jacob's Ladder, or the regions Naphtali and Zebulon that Jesus described as places of darkness and shadow of death.

When we think about Heaven or hell, we have images in our minds about them, but the spiritual reality is very different from Hollywood movies, the stories written by Dante Alighieri, or the paintings of the Renaissance. Therefore, God is changing our understanding and revelation, according to the apostolic and prophetic anointing under which we are living.

In traditional theology, there is little understanding of the invisible world and its operation. These theologies were developed in a time before the prophetic and apostolic anointings of today. After the Church fathers died at the end of the first century, much of the understanding they had was buried with them, especially the prophetic and the apostolic. Many important documents are probably still lost in history, and the ones we have today were gathered until the fourth century. Darkness covered the

Church for centuries until the reformation movement in the sixteenth century. From that time on and throughout each period of the history of the church, the light of revelation has been increasing.

With the restoration of the prophetic and apostolic movement in the last 20 years we are getting more understanding than in the prior centuries.

In spite of the little revelation that we have on these subjects, there are some theological points on which most Christians are agreed: We understand that hell is the eternal dwelling of the lost. We believe that the deceased either go to Heaven or hell. We are also aware that there is a lake of fire into which the beast and the false prophet will be thrown along with the condemned, after the great judgment of God. We know there is a place called *Tartarus* that is the deepest prison of hell (where the fallen angels dwell according to the Epistle of Jude). This is basically all the theology currently available on the subject.

Theology is developed on the basis of the Scripture, but many of the theologies we have today ignore and suppress the parts of Scripture that they didn't understand. This is why God is bringing a new reformation and understanding so we can grab hold of *everything* that is in the Bible for us.

However, God is revealing to many prophets and apostles concepts in the Spirit requiring deeper study. The Scriptures speak of invisible dimensions that affect each one of us. The Bible has many interesting verses concerning the regions of captivity, the way they operate, and where they are found. It is now that the Holy Spirit is shedding light on this subject for our understanding.

KNOWING THE SPIRIT WORLD: THE PROPHETIC ANOINTING

To understand the spiritual world, we must examine the prophetic anointing. In this manner, we can receive complete revelation. The prophetic anointing is beyond saying: "Thus saith the Lord," or having a vision from Heaven. *The prophetic anointing occurs in a different realm than ours. It is the entrance to the invisible Kingdom of God. It's the instrument used by God to make the Kingdom visible, audible, and palpable.* The prophetic anointing allows us to penetrate the Kingdom and extract from it riches of wisdom and knowledge.

The Old Testament prophets experienced this dimension. Some of them penetrated it, being caught away as Ezekiel was when he saw the temple of God and the Holy City. Daniel was lifted between Heaven and earth to receive the vision of the beasts. Moses was taken to extraordinary dimensions in which he received the revelation of the Genesis of creation.

The Book of Hebrews says that God has prepared something even better for us. Can't you see? God wants to give us greater things than He gave to these Old Testament people of God. The apostles understood this dimension because they penetrated the Kingdom of God. *The union of Heaven and earth through Jesus was their daily experience.*

For example, in the Book of Acts, Philip was translated from one place to another in both spirit and body (see Acts 8:39-40). The same thing happened to Peter, when he was taken prisoner by Herod. While in prison, he fell into a deep sleep and saw an angel who came to rescue him. Both of them translated through the prison, as if it were a mere vision. What was happening in the spiritual realm was simultaneously happening in the natural (see Acts 12:6-10). Paul was taken to the third heaven and didn't know whether he was in his body or outside his body (see 2 Cor. 12:2). John was taken in the Spirit to see the unfolding of the Book of Revelation in which Heaven and the depths of hell were revealed to him.

Dear reader, the Book of Acts did not end in the first century. It continues to be written through those who believe God and have penetrated the Kingdom of God.

How can we do this? Simply by following the example of the apostle John and others who practiced *being in the Spirit,* or entering the realm of His glory, as an essential part of their spiritual lives. Being in the Spirit is a state of deep intimacy with God through which the spirit of man becomes hypersensitive to the presence of God. This is the position from which revelation and visions of the heavenly Kingdom are seen in full.

The Kingdom of God is among us; only a thin, transparent membrane separates us from it. When we know God intimately, that membrane breaks. Our faith and love of God and time spent alone with Him allow us to pass to the other side. There, He becomes visible and audible and gives us great revelations.

The apostle John experienced extraordinary trances in which he saw Jesus in His glory. John was not only taken to the third heaven, but regions of the kingdom of darkness were also shown to him. Likewise, the more *we* experience Heaven and are used to inhabiting its reality, the greater revelations we will have, even about the secret places of our enemy.

John saw the spiritual regions mentioned in this book while being in God's presence. He was taken to Heaven in order to see what was to happen in the future. Beginning in Revelation 13, John sees one spiritual region after another, starting with "the sea." This was not an ocean on earth, but a spiritual ocean, where he observed the emergence of the beast. Please note that he was in Heaven watching the kingdom of darkness.

> *And the dragon stood on the shore of the sea. And I saw a beast coming out of the sea. He had ten horns and seven heads, with ten crowns on his horns, and on each head a blasphemous name* (Revelation 13:1).

Everything the beast does on the earth was revealed to John at *"the sea."* Afterward, he was shown a place between earth and hell, in order to see the second beast arise.

Then I saw another beast, coming out of the earth. He had two horns like a lamb, but he spoke like a dragon (Revelation 13:11).

In Revelation 17, an angel carried John to a place of darkness called *"the desert,"* where satan governs from Babylon. John described this spiritual city as a habitation of demons, the hideout of every unclean spirit, and the lodging of every unclean and abominable bird (see Rev. 18:2).

*One of the seven angels who had the seven bowls came and said to me, "Come, I will show you the punishment of the great prostitute, who sits on many waters....Then the angel carried me away **in the Spirit into a desert**. There I saw a woman sitting on a scarlet beast that was covered with blasphemous names and had seven heads and ten horns* (Revelation 17:1,3).

Jesus also spoke of that desert and taught his disciples that demons inhabit dry, desert places.

When an evil spirit comes out of a man, it goes through arid places seeking rest and does not find it (Matthew 12:43).

Another place revealed to John was "the Abyss or Abaddon" where satan is imprisoned for a thousand years and smoke and locusts are released to destroy the earth (see Rev. 20:1-3 and 9:2-3). Later, we will understand that these places are not only very important in the prophetic account of Revelation, but they are active places around us. Thousands of souls are held captive there while satan carries out his plans of tyranny and destruction.

The fifth angel sounded his trumpet, and I saw a star that had fallen from the sky to the earth. The star was given the key to the shaft of the Abyss. When he opened the Abyss,

*smoke rose from it like the smoke from a gigantic furnace.
The sun and sky were darkened by the smoke from the
Abyss....They had as king over them the angel of the Abyss,
whose name in Hebrew is Abaddon, and in Greek, Apol-
lyon* (Revelation 9:1-2;11).

(Abaddon is both the name of the angel and of the place, as we will
learn later.) During the revelation of the final judgment, God showed
John the places where death operates. Everyone who dies without Jesus
is taken to one of three different places, where they lie until they are
judged:

The sea *gave up the dead that were in it, and* ***death and
Hades*** *gave up the dead that were in them, and each
person was judged according to what he had done. Then
death and Hades were thrown into the lake of fire. The
lake of fire is the second death* (Revelation 20:13-14).

If we read that the dead are in the sea, we might think it refers to
people who have drowned or were eaten by sharks. If this were true, we
would read: "the sea gave up its dead and the earth gave up those who
were within it." But it doesn't mention "the earth," only the sea, death,
and Hades, which are three spiritual places.

The experience of the apostle John reveals to us both the heavenly
places and the regions of darkness. God wants us to have this type of
experience so He can give His children greater wisdom. *"No eye has seen,
no ear has heard, no mind has conceived what God has prepared for those
who love Him"* (1 Cor. 2:9).

Jesus came to make Heaven a visible, audible, and palpable reality.
Although the Holy Spirit will not take everyone to the third heaven,
everyone can have visions of the Kingdom of God and it is possible that
the Lord will reveal places of captivity to them:

having made known to us the mystery of His will, accord-
ing to His good pleasure which He purposed in Himself,
that in the dispensation of the fullness of the times He
might gather together in one all things in Christ, both
which are in heaven and which are on earth—in Him
(Ephesians 1:9-10 NKJV).

Seeing spiritual reality was common among the apostles. In the Book of Acts, the Apostle Peter clearly identified spiritual regions where Simon the magician was being held captive (see Acts 8:9-23). In this case, a vision was not necessary to identify the regions; the Holy Spirit revealed them through a word of knowledge.

This magician had accepted the Lord, was a baptized Christian, and took part in his local church, but he had never been set free. His mind was captured in the spiritual world. That is why he committed the mistake of trying to buy the gift of the Holy Spirit. In witchcraft, it is customary to purchase "spiritual services" with money. Peter rebuked him sharply.

Peter said to him, Destruction overtake your money and
you, because you imagined you could obtain the [free] gift
of God with money! You have neither part nor lot in this
matter, for your heart is all wrong in God's sight [it is not
straightforward or right or true before God]. So repent of
this depravity and wickedness of yours and pray to the
Lord that, if possible, this contriving thought and purpose
of your heart may be removed and disregarded and for-
given you. For I see that you are in the gall of bitterness
and in a bond forged by iniquity [to fetter souls] (Acts
8:20-23 AMP).

This Scripture describes clearly the apostle's ability to discern the condition of people's souls.

God is allowing thousands to see and understand the spiritual world in a deeper way, through the gifts of the word of knowledge and prophecy. In this way, we will be more effective in setting people free from captivity with extraordinary results.

These gifts operate at different levels. God permits prophets more vivid experiences than others. Some will be introduced to great depths, as the apostle Paul said, *"Whether in the body or out of the body, I don't know, I know a man who was taken to the third heaven"* (see 2 Cor. 12:2).

Amen.

TRANCE IN GOD VERSUS ASTRAL PROJECTION

As we continue to examine the prophetic dimensions, questions arise such as, "Is a trance in the Spirit the same thing as an astral projection?" Not at all! They are two very different things.

A trance is a vision in which one experiences the event in the spiritual world. It is as though you were in a movie theater watching a film and suddenly jumped into the big screen. The person having this experience is totally conscious, never leaving the physical body.

The Bible says that the spirit of the prophet is subject to the prophet (see 1 Cor. 14:32). In other words, the prophet can stop the experience voluntarily and is able to communicate with others who are having the same experience in the room (in the case of what is called a *corporate vision*). A vision is primarily a manifestation of the gifts of prophecy and word of knowledge. An example of this was described by the prophet Ezekiel who said that in visions of God he was taken to the holy city (see Ezekiel 40).

Again, this experience is an aspect of *being in the spirit*. It happens to a person developed in revelation gifts. John's and Paul's experiences can best be described as *translation in the Spirit*, or moving supernaturally from one place to another. Paul described the experience as a state of not knowing whether he was in the body or outside it (see 2 Cor. 12:3). *God is the only one capable of spiritually translating someone in this way. It is not accomplished by an act of the human will.*

What is known as *astral projection* in the occult world is a very different experience.

Astral projection (or astral travel) is an esoteric interpretation of any form of out-of-body experience (OOBE) that assumes the existence of an "astral body" separate from the physical body and capable of traveling outside it.[1] Astral projection or travel denotes the astral body leaving the physical body to travel in the astral plane.

After having been in the occult before my conversion to Christ and after 25 years as an authority in deliverance, I understand very well the difference between the real experience in God and this demonic practice.

In this occult experience the spirit of the traveler is surrendered to "guiding spirits" or "spirits of power" that separate the body from the spirit. After leaving the body, the person remains unconscious, in a lethargic state. He or she does not have the ability to control the experience, but is controlled by demons. It is possible for demon spirits to use the person's body to speak during the trance. The voice is clearly identified as belonging to someone other than the person who is traveling spiritually. This is an extremely dangerous practice and is contrary to the Bible.

Like all demonic experiences in the spiritual realm, astral projection is a counterfeit of the beneficial spiritual experiences that God has designed for us.

ENDNOTE

1. "Out-of-body experience", http://en.wikipedia.org/wiki/Out-of-body_experience.

Chapter 6

The Different Regions of Captivity

S piritual prisons are divided into different zones inside of the kingdom of evil. The fragmented soul is brought to these regions so the
designs of the devil can be manifested in the person's life.

I repeat: A soul may belong to God (being saved and redeemed) yet
suffer demonic influence because fragments of the soul are held captive.
This condition produces illness, failure, fear, anguish, and breakdowns
that do not respond to prayer. So let's examine these zones of captivity.

THE PLACE OF DARKNESS

Darkness is not only the generic name of the devil's empire; it is also
a spiritual place. As I mentioned before, the places are spiritual, they
exist in an invisible realm. Some can be located over a geographical area,
others are not.

> *The people who walked in darkness have seen a great
> light; those who dwelt in the land of the shadow of death,
> upon them a light has shined* (Isaiah 9:2 NKJV).

> *Now when Jesus had heard that John was cast into prison,
> he departed into Galilee; and leaving Nazareth, he came*

and dwelt in Capernaum, which is upon the sea coast, in the borders of Zabulon and Nephthalim: That it might be fulfilled which was spoken by Esaias the prophet, saying, The land of Zabulon, and the land of Nephthalim, by the way of the sea, beyond Jordan, Galilee of the Gentiles; The people which sat in darkness saw great light; and to them which sat in the region and shadow of death light is sprung up (Matthew 4:12-16 KJV).

This land of darkness and the shadow of death mentioned in these Scriptures was physically located in Zebulun and Naphtali. Jesus identified these spiritual regions in that specific zone, not in any other, revealing that every one of the cities of the earth can be ruled by a certain area of satan's empire.

It is important to mention that many other places could be under this influence of darkness and shadow of death, besides these Galilean cities.

*Nevertheless the **dimness** [darkness] shall not be such as was in **her vexation**, when at first He lightly **afflicted** the land of Zebulun and the land of Naphtali, and afterward did more grievously afflict her by the way of the sea, beyond Jordan, in Galilee of the nations* (Isaiah 9:1 KJV).

Darkness is established in certain places creating violence, affliction, anguish, and confusion among people living in those areas.

*Have regard for your covenant, because **haunts of violence fill the dark places** of the land* (Psalms 74:20).

Tell us what we should say to Him; we cannot draw up our case because of our darkness (Job 37:19).

The next psalm, written by one of the sons of Korah, a Levite, describes a spiritual place in which he is imprisoned with no way out.

*Thou hast laid me in the lowest pit, in **darkness**, in the deeps. Thy wrath lieth hard upon me, and Thou hast **afflicted** me with all thy waves. Selah. Thou hast put away mine acquaintance far from me; Thou hast made me an abomination unto them: **I am shut up, and I cannot come forth*** (Psalms 88:6-8 KJV).

The Lord reveals many levels of darkness while setting captives free. In actual ministry situations in which we enter these regions, we ask the Lord to shine His light to enable us to see despite the darkness there. Many times, we need angels of intense light to open the way for us to move forward.

The people who are trapped in these places stumble around as though they were blind. People live in constant doubt and unbelief because they cannot see. Their eyes are in complete darkness. This darkness not only symbolizes living in sin but also the idea of not knowing where to go, what to do, or what one's purpose is. There are people who have repented, yet are still in darkness as far as many situations in their lives are concerned.

*Like the blind we grope along the wall, feeling our way like men without eyes. At midday **we stumble as if it were twilight**; among the strong, we are like the dead* (Isaiah 59:10).

This region could be described as a place full of holes in the ground. People trip, and when they fall, their souls are afflicted in these places. There are narrow pits of oppression and suffocation.

In the natural world, these people seem dark and oppressed. Everything about them is narrow: their vision, their way of thinking, and even the way they walk and move. If you observe them, they appear bound by invisible cords. Their body language clearly displays their captivity. They prefer dark places and are hoarders. They are generally (though not always) people who lack any semblance of order in their lives or houses.

Lack of order speaks of darkness and it systematically attracts them. It hearkens back to the time in Genesis, when the earth was formless and void and darkness covered it.

Job also made the connection between a lack of order and darkness:

> *to the land of deepest night, of deep shadow and disorder,*
> *where even the light is like darkness* (Job 10:22).

A life that is without order and out of alignment with God's priorities clearly demonstrates captivity in the regions of darkness.

The prisons in this place are like deep caves, many of them are as labyrinths that lead to dungeons. In the book *Healing the Wounded Spirit*, by John and Paula Sanford, John (one of the most prominent deliverance ministers in the United States) describes an interesting deliverance from the region of darkness. Jo, the person he set free, lived as though she were dead inside. John, after trying every form of deliverance, was led in a vision to a place where the devil held her captive:

> I "saw" our wonderful Lord walking down a steeply sloping dark tunnel. He did not carry a torch or lantern. He was himself the light. I followed Him. The experience was much like following a car down a narrow lane at night, watching the headlights momentarily shine on the walls or bushes, leaving darkness behind. I watched the light of Jesus illuminate the walls as He passed. We came to a huge dungeon door, ancient and rusted, locked. Before the Lord, it opened by itself. Scriptures raced through my mind, "*...behold, I am alive forevermore and I have the keys of death and Hades*" (Revelation 1:18 NKJV). He hadn't needed to insert a key; He himself is the key! The door flew open at the authority. "*The gates of hell shall not prevail against it*" (Matthew 16:18b KJV). It was confirmed to me in a flash, that Jesus meant to speak of the Church on the attack, not on the defensive, breaking

open the gates of Hell to invade and set its captives free! **We were entering a dungeon of Hell, and I knew it!** [emphasis added]

I watched as He walked across a dirty floor. Phantasmagoria of Hell fled before His presence! There in a corner, huddled in a fetal position, manacled by wrists and ankles attached by chains to a wall, was Jo. She appeared ghastly white and blue, emaciated and starved, tiny as a child. With His beautiful nail-scarred brown hands, He deftly, gently broke the shackles off of Jo. He picked her up, cradling her softly against His chest and I thought, *"He shall feed His flock like a shepherd: He shall gather the lambs with his arm, and carry them in his bosom, and shall gently lead those that are with young"* (Isaiah 40:11 KJV). I wept for joy at the beauty of it.

The Lord carried Jo out of that place. I described aloud for Jo what I was seeing. Later, she told me that she felt every moment of it in indescribable joy and anticipation.

As He carried her, He breathed His own breath into her, while Genesis 2:7 and countless Scriptures about the wind of the Holy Spirit (as in John 3), and Elisha breathing his breath into the Shunamite woman's dead son (see 2 Kings 4:18-37), cascaded through my mind. Then, He set her on her feet and taking her left hand in His right, began to walk out of the tunnel with her. As they walked, Jo began to grow, like the WonderBread advertisement of some years ago, from a little girl to the grown woman she is. Then He passed His hands over her body and wherever I could see skin, it turned from deathly pale to glowing pink.

The vision ended as I saw Him turn her loose to frolic in the lovely meadow, as He watched, beaming with joy and pride.[1]

Jo was in one of these deep holes where the devil sucked the life and joy out of her. These deep pits in the regions of darkness make up different kinds of jails. In some, the people are tormented by demons of fear. These manifest as horrible spirits, beings with their flesh eaten away, spirits of perdition and homicide. In the natural world, these people are afraid of the dark and cannot sleep in a dark room. They feel as if something in the darkness is stalking them. They are always fearful that something unexpected and catastrophic could happen to them. This happens because this is what the trapped piece of their soul is literally experiencing in its place of captivity.

In general, when we are delivering people like this, we are first introduced through regions of fear, where the soul was fragmented by a terrifying incident or trauma. Fragmentation could also have occurred due to participation in the occult by ancestors or by the individual to whom we are ministering.

Media contribute to these issues. Many horror movies are made with the purpose of trapping souls. Some time ago, we held a spiritual warfare offensive at Disney World, Universal Studios, and other amusement parks in the Orlando, Florida, area.

We were astounded to see so many rides whose purpose was to fill people with fear. But that was not all we saw; in many of the rides, at the moment of greatest fear, the voice of a demon or monster could be heard shouting, "Now, I am possessing your soul," or, "Your soul is mine for eternity." Do you think this is just a harmless game? Those who have ears to hear, let them hear!

Thousands of people leave these parks with pale faces caused by terror. They laugh nervously, totally ignorant of the devil's devices. The Lord revealed to us the spiritual prisons of darkness in those places of

Revenge of the Mummy

apparent amusement and we cried in deep intercession to set the millions of souls free who have remained captive there.

Another type of prison in the region of darkness is sin. Spiritual regions are not isolated. For example, when a person suffers from intense trauma, regions of fear capture his or her soul. As fearful circumstances increase during the person's lifetime, the soul sinks into deeper levels that we will discuss later. In general, the Holy Spirit reveals the soul's final place of captivity.

Prisons of sin look like cells. Sometimes they look like valleys of chained people, whipped by demons who coerce them to sin again and again. Many are located in muddy lakes of sexual filth and perversion surrounded by grotesque demons of sensuality. We have seen people who are forced to drink without ceasing in lakes of alcohol, and others who are forced to drug themselves continually in their prison cells. Flames of fire arise from the bottom of the prison, violently burning the soul. This is the extreme case of someone who cannot get out.

We are all responsible for our sins, because free will is always ours and not the devil's. I am referring to cases of true possession in which the person has repented many times and inevitably sins again. We should be careful and use discernment in these instances, because some people who say they have repented really love to sin. In this case, we should lead the person to an encounter with the sacrifice of Jesus on the cross, to feel Jesus' pain for his or her sin.

The regions of darkness are diverse. It is not the intention of this book to exalt the habitations of satan; rather, the point is to expose them. Of all the places of captivity, the ones that make the strongest impression on me are the prisons of homosexuality. In this region, the sexes are confused. It is a whirlwind of sexes mixed together. Men are put in prisons formed in the shape of the male organ; women are housed within the female organ. In this way, the captives become homosexuals and lesbians. The people I saw incarcerated inside those prisons were totally consumed by those gigantic organs. They were unable to see the opposite sex in order to function in the way God had designed them.

The Lord has permitted me to deliver people from homosexuality and, I am happy to say, their lives have changed radically. One young man shares his testimony in Chapter 9.

GATES OF DARKNESS

The region of "darkness" with its prisons, labyrinths, valleys, and abysses is a zone connected to other regions. Normally, the following listed places are front gates of entry.

Regions of Fear

These regions and demons are guards and are responsible for bringing the prisoners from the regions of darkness. When a person's soul is terrorized by some extreme event, this gate opens and the fragmented soul is taken captive.

Covenant Chambers

Occult ceremonies performed in the natural world open gates in the spiritual world. Some gates have their origin in sorcery, witchcraft, divination, rituals of idolatry, Masonic rituals, mind control, and all kinds of New Age rituals.

The Gates of Pain

Gates open after a soul suffers deep pain, such as the loss of a loved one, rejection, or abandonment. It may also occur when the soul, as a fetus, suffers an attempted abortion. Treasons, humiliations, or insults lead the broken soul into captivity. They are led through pain to regions of darkness such as the captivities of hatred, anger, revenge, violence, and resentment, where they are afflicted and tormented.

Examples of the Path of Captivity
(Different in every case)

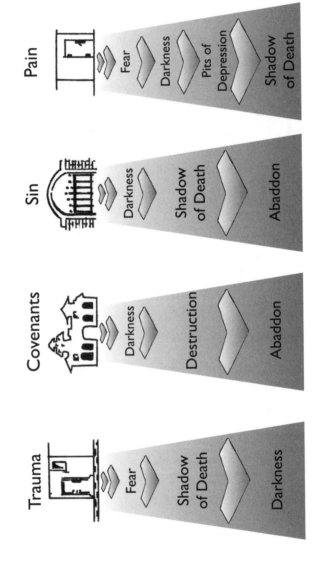

THE ABYSS, PITS, AND DEEP PLACES

In each of the regions of captivity, there are prisons, pits, and turbid currents of muddy waters. All of these can be found in the regions of darkness, in the Abyss, in Abaddon, and in the shadow of death. Spiritual holes serve as traps to capture prey. The soul drowns in despair feeling helpless and unable to escape.

> *They spread a net for my feet—I was bowed down in distress. **They dug a pit** in my path—but they have fallen into it themselves* (Psalms 57:6).

The Abyss is a place close to hell or Sheol. It is equivalent to the word "Infernos" in Latin, that also mean an inferior plane.[2] It is the place of the waters of darkness. Water spirits are sent out from there, such as Leviathan, the prince of pride.

> *In that day, the Lord will punish with His sword, His fierce, great and powerful sword, Leviathan the gliding serpent, Leviathan the coiling serpent; He will slay the monster of the sea* (Isaiah 27:1).

> *Yet you shall be brought down to Sheol, to the lowest depths of the Pit* (Isaiah 14:15 NKJV).

The Abyss is, without a doubt, one of the gates of hell. It is from this place that "the beast" of Revelation comes out. The Bible helps identify one of its main entrances, known as the face of the Abyss. This place is located under the ice in the polar regions, where there is no dry land. As I said before, some can be located on a physical plane but not all of them.

> *when the waters become hard as stone, when the surface of the deep* [Abyss] *is frozen* (Job 38:30).

In 2004, the Lord led us on a spiritual warfare expedition to the North Pole, before this Scripture in Job had been revealed to me. The Lord inspired me to fight the powers of darkness that were affecting some European countries from that location.

We were walking through an enormous valley of frozen water, when my spirit began to hear shouts and voices coming from under the ice. At that moment, the Lord opened my spiritual eyes and I saw thousands of people held captive in a bottomless pit. Spirits of insanity then burst forth from that place and were released upon the earth.

In that moment, one of our warriors came under an attack of death. His life began to leave him by the second. The Lord directed us to hold him up so he wouldn't fall. My husband, Emerson, and I dragged him away from that place. The Spirit exhorted us to persist in prayer in order to prevent the devil from imprisoning this man's soul. After awhile, we were victorious. We returned from the North Pole unharmed, but the memory of what we had seen and experienced was continually on our minds.

Soon afterward, Apostle Fernando Orihuela, from Bolivia, told me that the Holy Spirit had been revealing to him the importance of the poles in the spiritual world. The Holy Spirit had shown him that the entrance to the face of the Abyss was at the North Pole. When he told me this, what we had gone through there made much more sense.

The Abyss is made up of deep pits of water. Souls are trapped in some of the pits; in others are demons that are waiting to be loosed when the fifth trumpet is blown, as described in the Book of Revelation:

> *The fifth angel sounded his trumpet, and I saw a star that had fallen from the sky to the earth. The star was given the key to the shaft of the Abyss. When he opened **the Abyss**, smoke rose from it like the smoke from a gigantic furnace. The sun and sky were darkened by the smoke from the Abyss. And out of the smoke locusts came down upon the*

earth and were given power like that of scorpions of the earth (Revelation 9:1-3).

Pits of the Abyss and Muddy Pits

*Save me, O God, for the waters have come up to my neck. I sink in the **miry depths**, where there is no foothold. I have come into the **deep waters**; the floods engulf me.... Do not let the floodwaters engulf me or the depths* [Abyss] *swallow me up or **the pit** close its mouth over me* (Psalms 69:1-2,15).

During the Davidic times in which portions of the Book of Psalms were written, the prophets in the tabernacle of David understood the spiritual realm well. They saw and experienced many of the same things that God is revealing to us today. When we enter prophetic worship, the gifts of the Spirit begin to flow and detailed visions appear before our eyes.

The psalmists who wrote the types of songs seen in Psalm 69 were not writing poetry. These are prayers of spiritual warfare, led by God in a specific manner and with great understanding.

The "miry pits" have to do with the mud of iniquity. They are traps created by the enemy, situations where someone is tangled in a net of iniquity and cannot escape. In the natural world, this is going to show up through difficult situations. It may be a business deal gone wrong creating legal situations, binding the person's hands. These are circumstances designed to bring destruction. The persons may feel like they are drowning and can't find an answer.

Pits of Desperation

I WAITED patiently and expectantly for the Lord; and He inclined to me and heard my cry. He drew me up out

of a horrible pit [a pit of tumult and of destruction], out
of the miry clay (froth and slime), and set my feet upon
a rock, steadying my steps and establishing my goings
(Psalms 40:1-2 AMP).

Many people who fall into depression are held captive in a pit. The Lord rescued me from a psychiatric hospital, where my shattered soul had been trapped in pits seemingly without exit. I clearly felt myself sinking further and further into a deep, dark hole. The voices of the devil tormented me day and night. Visions of horrible beings harassed me all the time. My spirit and soul lived in the depths of a desolate, terribly sad place. I had vivid nightmares every night. The doctors called it schizophrenia. Today, I know differently. I was experiencing captivity in my soul. I felt bound and imprisoned by invisible walls that smothered me. I felt as though I could hardly breathe.

When God rescued me and Jesus genuinely entered my heart, I literally saw the door of the vault-like iron prison open. I saw myself moving into a spacious place, full of light and peace.

*He brought me out into a **spacious place**; He rescued me*
because He delighted in me (2 Samuel 22:20).

The places of Heaven are spacious. The Spirit rises and soars. Our vision expands and becomes clear. Peace and joy are everywhere.

I had to remain firm in order to keep my freedom. I remember, at the beginning of my Christian life, how the devil suggested again and again that I dive into one of those pits of affliction. His words were depressing, reminding me of the pain I had suffered. It was like standing on a slippery slope where it was hard to keep my footing. Many times, I saw that pit clearly. It invited me to jump in. The devil pushed me with great force, but my will was mine and I was not going to surrender it to the devil. My willpower served as a rudder and kept me in Jesus' arms. While sitting in His lap one day, I heard His voice say to me, "Shut the mouth of the Abyss! I have the authority to close it, and I am giving it to you!"

The Different Regions of Captivity

So I did it. Now, it doesn't matter how sad my circumstances are, that pit is closed and it can no longer swallow me. Hallelujah!

Our will is a powerful weapon. Surrender it to God and exercise the power of decision, always choosing the ways of the Lord. Stop believing that the devil is almighty; he is not.

The Pit of Destruction

But Thou, O God, shalt bring them down into the pit of destruction: bloody and deceitful men shall not live out half their days; but I will trust in Thee (Psalms 55:23 KJV).

Although there are pits of eternal perdition, there are also those that hold people imprisoned in sin, vices, and evil actions. I have seen people whose entire minds are held captive in this place. Almost all of their inner doors have been taken over by demons and their captive minds receive the designs of the devil with great clarity. This is the case with sorcerers, those in the mafia, drug traffickers, thieves, and serial killers.

The Pit of Corruption and the Pit of Iniquity

*Behold, for peace I had great bitterness: but Thou hast in love to my soul delivered it from **the pit of corruption**: for Thou hast cast all my sins behind thy back* (Isaiah 38:17 KJV).

Simon the magician, about whom I wrote earlier, was held captive in this pit.

*For I perceive that thou art in the **gall of bitterness, and in the bond of iniquity*** (Acts 8:23 KJV).

85

In countries with a lot of corruption, these pits operate at a national level. The consciousness of the people is totally influenced by these places.

> *The nations have fallen in the pit they have dug; their feet are caught in the net they have hidden* (Psalms 9:15).

In my country, Mexico, this is quite evident. We frequently witness people operating in corrupt ways, without remorse. Bribing policemen to avoid paying fines, lying, stealing, and taking advantage of others are common practices, even among Christians. The worst thing is they don't realize it in many cases. It is normal to them. This is from the very pit of corruption and we must remove our souls from those places.

Every one of us, as sons and daughters of God (if that is who we are) has the ability to call out our own soul from captivity. God has given you the power to overcome the gates of hell. You have the keys of the Kingdom of God to open every prison door where you may be held captive. Open them! Command your soul to leave those places. You don't belong there. You are of God and must position yourself in heavenly places.

The whole of creation is enslaved in those regions. That is why it is so important to understand who we are in God and our mission as liberators:

> *because the creation itself also will be delivered from the bondage of corruption into the glorious liberty of the children of God* (Romans 8:21 NKJV).

PLACES OF DEATH

This is a very interesting part of our study because these places of death—Sheol, the Valley of the Shadow of Death, and the Region of Death—constitute one of Jesus' most important victories.

Many times we think the work of the cross ended when the Messiah gave up His Spirit on Calvary. However, He descended to the lowest parts of the earth to finish His work.

In Gethsemane, He conquered the soul's pain and the fear of death. This took more than three hours. Between His captivity, judgment, and crucifixion, fewer than 24 hours passed. But in the deepest parts of the earth where He conquered hell, death, and the regions of our captivity, it took three days. This is very important for us to consider.

Jesus did not just die for us. The how, when, and where of His death and burial are very significant. Every part of His suffering had a purpose. They are all part of the complete design for our redemption. Before the foundation of the world, He was spiritually slain to redeem our spirit (Revelation 13:8).

With the pain of His soul, He paid for our pain. In His body, he took sickness and iniquity. Stripped of His clothing, He exposed sin; through death, He conquered death.

> Since the children have flesh and blood, He too shared in their humanity so that **by His death He might destroy him** who holds the power of death—that is, the devil... (Hebrews 2:14).

It was necessary for Jesus to be sacrificed on Passover because he was the Lamb of God. It had to happen on top of a mountain, Calvary, to take the power of high places from the devil. It was also relevant that His body be put in a cave covered by a rock, because Jesus not only conquered the heights, but also the deepest parts of the earth. An exhaustive study of every part of His passion yields impressive information. I have analyzed this subject in my book *Eat My Flesh, Drink My Blood*. For now, I will only focus on His death.

As we said before, death is not our final destiny in this world. Death operates in the midst of the natural world in many ways: through fear, sickness, accidents, insanity, and everything that decays. In the spiritual

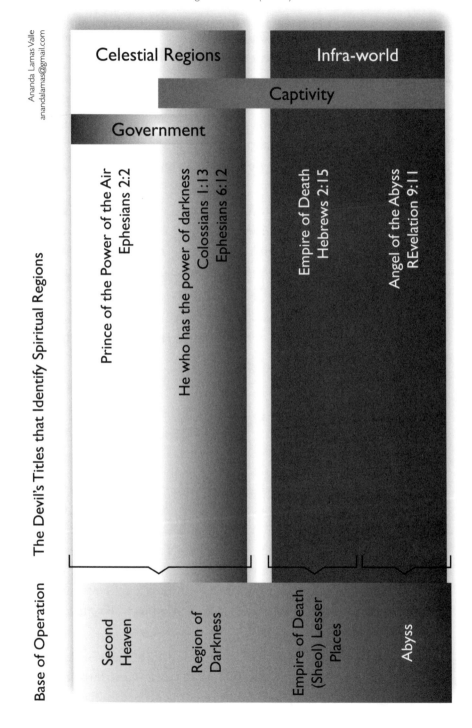

The Devil's Titles that Identify Spiritual Regions

Base of Operation

Celestial Regions

Infra-world

Captivity

Government

Prince of the Power of the Air
Ephesians 2:2

He who has the power of darkness
Colossians 1:13
Ephesians 6:12

Empire of Death
Hebrews 2:15

Angel of the Abyss
REvelation 9:11

Second
Heaven

Region of
Darkness

Empire of Death
(Sheol) Lesser
Places

Abyss

realm, death kills entire movements of the Spirit and destroys churches and ministries. Everything man does apart from God is death.

The topic of death makes most people nervous. This is because it is the method the devil uses to control this world.

There are carnal believers that have their heart in the things of this world. For them, death is a matter of fear. There are true Christians whose hearts are focused on heavenly things. For them, death is nothing more than the victory that unites us to our beloved Jesus. The person who learns to deny his or her own life, even if it means death, has overcome death and disarmed the devil and his empire. For these believers, this subject is not traumatic or scary, because they have conquered it. Unfortunately, many of our beloved brothers are still fighting and are held in captivity from which they must come out.

Sheol

As mentioned earlier, the Hebrew meaning for *Sheol* is, "lower places." In Greek, it is called *Hades* and in Latin it is *hell*. The word *hell* simply locates satan's base camp. Satan is *"the prince of the power of the air"* (Eph. 2:2). Under this title he controls the second heaven. He rules over captivity and death from the underworld.

No one objects to the concept of the devil governing the air, and no one argues with the idea of the second heaven influencing the earth. But now, God wants to increase our understanding over the enemy's operations base (Sheol) in order for us to destroy his work in every dimension.

The devil is not only the prince of the power of the air, but he also carries the titles "angel of the Abyss" (Rev. 9:11), "prince or ruler of darkness" (Eph. 6:12), and he who "holds the power of death" (Heb. 2:14). Therefore, to think of the spiritual world only in strict terms of Heaven and hell is a very limited perception.

The devil governs from the air and the mountaintops. In Sheol, or hell, he deals with captivity and death. The region of death has two parts, one is the dwelling of the dead, the second is the place of oppression used to torment the captured souls. From this place satan releases sickness, disease, and death.

As I previously said, *hell* and *infernal* are words we use to describe things that have to do with the devil. However, this is more a popular use of language than an accurate depiction.

Some countries, such as Poland, are reflections of the regions of death. In the year 2000, in order to open the heavens of that country, we led a spiritual warfare expedition. The Spirit revealed the nation had made covenants with the regions of death. The spiritual power over the nation was called *the Black Madonna.*

Her image can be found in the basement of the basilica of Jasna Góra, in the city of Czestochowa. It is a replica of the designs of hell. The chapel is painted black, and so is the "Madonna's" face, along with three scars on one of her cheeks. Her face was the map of Poland's destruction, established in hell. The history of Poland is a reflection of the face of the idol. The nation has been divided into three parts more than once.

In addition, there are crucifixes with the image of Jesus hanging from the cross set up throughout the nation. At first I thought it was a religious thing, but the Lord enlightened my understanding.

He told me, "The devil wants to see Me dead because that is the victory that he announces in hell, saying that he was the one who killed Me. Each one of these crucifixes is a territorial mark to establish death throughout the country. These are decrees that establish the region of Sheol upon the earth."

Poland has been devastated and destroyed many times in its history. In fact, Adolf Hitler chose this nation to build an altar to death itself. He studied the occult extensively. The devil asked him to reproduce a replica of hell on earth. The goal of every antichrist is to build an altar of death to govern the world.

Hitler's goal was to burn 6,666,000 Jews and Christians. This altar was built in Auschwitz, Poland. The German leader had more in mind

The Black Madonna, Poland

than simply killing the Jewish people. If that had been his only objective, he would have bombed the ghettos where he held them prisoner. Why transport them to one place? Why feed them and hold them captive? Why spend money and energy building camps with bedrooms, gas chambers, and crematories, if the only objective was to kill them?

The plan was more diabolical. He needed to reproduce the pain of hell with its sounds of agony and despair. He wanted to recreate the different levels of prisons and dungeons that existed in Sheol. From his soul of captivity he desired to reproduce the same narrow places, oppression, and feelings of suffocation he was experiencing.

In the deepest prison cells of Auschwitz, Hitler's captives were walled in alive. Sometimes it took as many as four days for them to die. Hitler delighted in hearing the music of Wagner and Beethoven mixed with his prisoners' screams of terror and pain coming from the gas chambers and torture rooms.

While all of this was happening, the empire of darkness extended over Europe. Captivity and the shadow of death were established on the continent.

It is horrifying to do massive deliverances of those in captivity from those nations. The pain of those who are trapped from their parents' experiences in the Second World War is heartrending. Opening the gates of their prisons and setting them free is both sad and joyful. Many times, health and healings are instantaneous.

Sheol is not only a place, it is also a power used by satan in order to take people into captivity. Hitler understood the power of Sheol. It does not only take captives during victimization, as in the case of the Jewish people during the war, but Sheol has an attraction power that causes people to become snared. In the following verses, I have highlighted the fact that the upright will rule over them to demonstrate that here the Bible is not speaking about people that are already dead. This passage is talking about people who are alive; however, death feeds on them

Bodies of woman and child

Bodies prepared for removal from Nazi death camp, Auschwitz, Poland.

Chambers where people were encased unto death.

Women and children at Nazi death camp, Auschwitz, Poland.

Nazi Death Camps, Auschwitz, Poland.

Crematories at Auschwitz death camp, Poland.

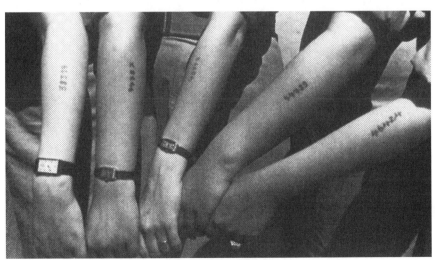

Nazi Death Camps, Auschwitz, Poland.

EXECUTIVE OFFICE OF THE PRESIDENT

☆WAR REFUGEE BOARD

WASHINGTON, D. C.

GERMAN EXTERMINATION CAMPS — AUSCHWITZ AND BIRKENAU

It is a fact beyond denial that the Germans have <u>deliberately</u> <u>and systematically murdered millions of innocent civilians - Jews</u> <u>and Christians alike</u> - all over Europe. This campaign of terror and brutality, which is unprecedented in all history and which even now continues unabated, is part of the German plan to subjugate the free peoples of the world.

So revolting and diabolical are the German atrocities that the minds of civilized people find it difficult to believe that they have actually taken place. But the governments of the United States and of other countries have evidence which clearly substantiates the facts.

The War Refugee Board is engaged in a desperate effort to save as many as possible of Hitler's intended victims. To facilitate its work the Board has representatives in key spots in Europe. These representatives have tested contacts throughout Europe and keep the Board fully advised concerning the German campaign of extermination and torture.

Recently the Board received from a representative close to the scene two eye-witness accounts of events which occurred in notorious extermination camps established by the Germans. The first report is based upon the experiences of two young Slovakian Jews who escaped in April, 1944 after spending two years in the Nazi concentration camps at Auschwitz and Birkenau in southwestern Poland. The second report is made by a non-Jewish Polish major, 4 the only survivor of one group imprisoned at Auschwitz.

[185]

U.S. Presidential Report on Nazi Death Camps.

"It is a fact beyond denial that the Germans have deliberately and systematically murdered millions of innocent civilians—Jews and Christians alike—all over Europe."

and Sheol is their dwelling. It is theologically incorrect to think that the saints rule over the dead.

> *They that trust in their wealth, and boast themselves in the multitude of their riches;... Like sheep they are laid in the grave; death shall feed on them. **The upright will have dominion over them** in the morning; and their beauty shall consume in the grave from their dwelling* (Psalms 49:6; 49:14 KJV).

The people in this passage live there in a spiritual sense, and death feeds on everything they do. The passage says you can see the place of their captivity written on their faces. We see it in their deadened gazing or violent looks. By contrast, David expresses hope:

> *But God will redeem my soul **from the power of the grave**: and He shall receive me. Selah* (Psalms 49:15 KJV).

Notice in the next passage that the soul of King David was captive in Sheol, which produced an illness that nearly killed him.

> *O Lord my God, I called to You for help and You healed me. O Lord, **You brought me up from the grave** [Sheol]; You spared me from going down into the pit* (Psalms 30:2-3).

(Please note that the Hebrew word translated "grave" in the New International Version and others, can also be translated "Sheol," as it is in the Amplified Bible.)

Believing lies or falsehood is a way of feeding on death. It makes you captive in the regions of death.

> *You boast, "We have entered into a covenant with death, with the grave we have made an agreement. When an overwhelming scourge sweeps by, it cannot touch us, for*

we have made a lie our refuge and falsehood our hiding place" (Isaiah 28:15).

The Valley of the Shadow of Death

This is the projection of things that move in the regions of death and Sheol on the earth.

The cords of the grave coiled around me; the snares of death confronted me (Psalms 18:5).

We understand that many illnesses are from regions like the Valley of the Shadow of Death, or Sheol.

In Psalm 23, we see that many Christians go through that valley and suffer the consequences of the journey. For some, the soul is taken captive and, if not rescued, will sink further and further until it dies.

*Even though I walk **through the valley of the shadow of death**, I will fear no evil, for You are with me; Your rod and Your staff, they comfort me* (Psalms 23:4).

It is a dangerous thing to be a patient in a hospital. People are unaware of the connection to the regions of death. In fact, most hospitals are built near cemeteries. There is spiritual activity from the regions of death located nearby. These places of intense suffering, trauma, pain, and death are designed to trap and capture unsuspecting persons.

If you must go to a hospital, you must immediately close the gates of death and Sheol and spiritually cut all the currents of death and the spiritual tunnels coming from the cemeteries.

In Jesus we have the keys of Sheol and death. The keys are used to close and open. In this case, we close the door and make a decree with the authority that Jesus has given each of us. Later in this book, we will discuss heavenly regions and learn why there is no reason for us, as children of God, to go to hospitals. God wants to spare us from that unnecessary suffering.

Not long ago, we conducted spiritual warfare in the city of Saint Augustine, Florida. Our ministry offices are located in the vicinity. Aside from being the oldest city in the United States, Saint Augustine is ranked the third most haunted city in the nation.

Death is the central theme of the city and its inhabitants, as illustrated by city attractions such as ghost tours. Families from around the world bring their children and babies to the cemeteries and haunted houses. All who visit, and especially the children, come face to face with real spirits. Night after night, dozens of people enter the regions of death to be held captive unawares.

We asked the Lord for a strategy to set this city free. The Lord revealed that the population was submerged in the region of the shadow of death. This is the most superficial part of Sheol and is found at ground level. It is also where poltergeist spirits roam and spiritualists invoke the spirits of the dead. This practice attracts spirits of death, which produce sickness and spiritual death among the population.

Some theologies teach that there is no such thing as spirits of dead people having contact with the living. The belief is that ghosts are demons that assume the form and voice of those who have departed. I also believed this until God opened my eyes during a battle in Rome, Italy.

We went to the Vatican to pray for the Catholic people in captivity. Praying in that place caused an intense battle to ensue. The Holy Spirit said to me, *"You are completely ignoring the army of the dead. They are coming against you. Mobilize my army of angels against them."* When I obeyed, I remembered that, in every mass, Catholics ask the dead to protect them.

Studying the subject in greater depth, I first consulted with the Holy Spirit and then with various theologians, asking them about Scriptures

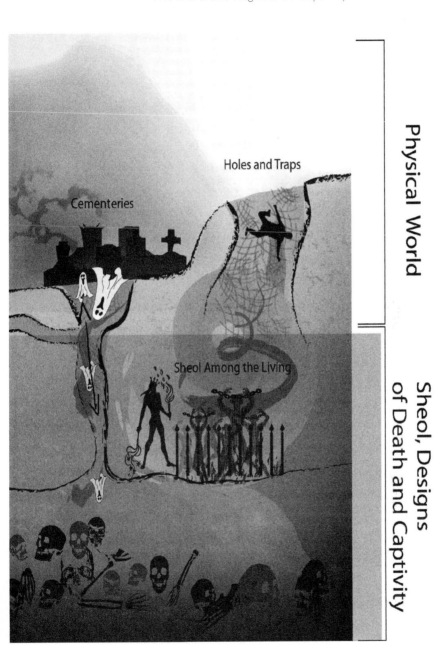

Physical World

Sheol, Designs
of Death and Captivity

Ananda Lamas Valle
anandalamas@gmail.com

that confirm the belief that ghosts are demons and not spirits of the dead.

They all came to the same conclusion: There are no such Scriptures. They admitted it was a practically unknown subject in Evangelical theology; however, they agreed that certain passages in the Bible seem to indicate that the dead can appear in the world of the living, as we will see in this section.

I arrived at the conclusion that, if the Scriptures do not affirm ghosts or spirits of the dead as being demons, why should we? We should scrutinize the Word of God to discover the truth.

I feel that in the matter of deliverance, it is important to know the difference between demons, ghosts, and spirits of the dead. Let's look at verses that support what the Lord has shown me:

> *And you shall be laid low [Jerusalem], speaking from beneath the ground, and your speech shall come humbly from the dust. And your voice shall be like that of a **ghost** [produced by a medium] coming from the earth, and your speech shall whisper and squeak as it chatters from the dust* (Isaiah 29:4 AMP).

In this Scripture, we see that the Lord uses the word *ghost* when referring to someone who is dead speaking from under the earth. Genesis 3:19 says, *"By the sweat of your brow you will eat your food until you return to the ground, since from it you were taken; for dust you are and to dust you will return."* Only a dead person goes to the dust, a demon doesn't.

Another verse that gives us light in this matter is found in the book of Job:

> *Fear came upon me, and trembling, which made all my bones to shake. Then a spirit passed before my face; the hair of my flesh stood up: It stood still, but I could not*

discern the form thereof: An image was before mine eyes,
there was silence, and I heard a voice, saying, Shall mor-
tal man be more just than God? shall a man be more pure
than his maker? (Job 4:15-17 KJV)

Job identifies the person speaking with him as a ghost.

The key is in the word *form* and the word *image*.[3]

The word *form* means something beautiful to see, a beautiful face. In other languages it is translated as a beautiful face. Nevertheless, it produced fear and Job's hair stood up. So we know it is not a demon by his appearance and his message. It is not an angel, either; the presence of an angel produces peace, reverence, even the fear of the Lord, which is different than being afraid of something. When the Bible wants to speak about an angel, it rather says the word *angel* or someone in the likeness of man, but never "a ghost."

So in the case of this Scripture, I believe it was a ghost, the disembodied spirit of a man, a phantom.

He had the face of a man, but it was not someone Job knew. He did not say that he was a demon or an angel.

The other word that is interesting to study in this same passage is "image."

The Hebrew word is *tmuwnah,* something portioned (i.e., fashioned) out, as a shape, that is (indefinitely) *phantom,* or (specifically) embodiment.[4]

As we have seen, both of the words point to the idea that it was truly a phantom and nothing indicates that it was a demon.

In another passage found in Psalms, King David prayed against the voices of the dead.

Let me not be put to shame, O Lord, for I have cried out
to You; but let the wicked be put to shame and lie silent in
the grave (Psalms 31:17).

If he has to pray for them to be silent, that means that there is a possibility that they could speak.

First Samuel 28 provides an example of invocation of spirits. King Saul asked the witch of Endor to call up the prophet Samuel's spirit. This is a sin. Conversation with the dead is an attempt of the devil to trap one's soul. This passage demonstrates that the dead are not demons, but human spirits.

> *And the king said unto her, Be not afraid: for what sawest thou? And the woman said unto Saul, I saw gods ascending out of the earth. And he said unto her, What form is he of? And she said, An old man cometh up; and he is covered with a mantle. And Saul perceived that it was Samuel, and he stooped with his face to the ground, and bowed himself. And Samuel said to Saul, Why hast thou disquieted me, to bring me up?...* (1 Samuel 28:13-15a KJV)

We find here the one that came up from among the dead was the prophet Samuel. Perhaps the psychic saw him as a spirit full of the splendor of God, since she confused him with a god, but it was certainly not a demon in disguise.

Now, let's return to the story of the haunted city of Saint Augustine. I asked the Holy Spirit how to pray against the ghosts that wandered in this zone of the shadow of death, since they are not demons. He said, *"Order My angels to take them captive to their eternal dwellings."* We did it, and immediately they were taken prisoner and to deep regions of death. The atmosphere in the city changed dramatically, and one can no longer feel the presence of death like before.

In the place of the shadow of death, the devil has the designs to destroy the spiritual life of churches, movements of God, and ministers. At times, I have heard the expression: "This city is a cemetery for pastors." In other words, the region of death is established over that city, and the result is that many things die—businesses, marriages, and even churches.

In 2003, I was invited to El Rey Jesús Church, a growing church in Miami. Pastor Guillermo Maldonado told me he was worried because every church that grew to 1,500 members in the city had been dramatically destroyed. He told me of several church leaders who had fallen into sin after their congregations reached the 1,500 membership. Their ministries and their churches had been decimated. I explained the designs of hell, and we agreed to pray to discover the design of death over the city.

Through a vision, the Lord took us to one of the regions of Sheol. There we saw demons allied with witches, who had built a cemetery for pastors in the spiritual world. The objective of this cemetery was to kill the spiritual life of God's servants. We saw gravestones with the names of every pastor who ministered in Miami, and among them was Pastor Maldonado. In the Spirit, we removed the tombs and opened the prisons. One by one, we released the ministers. Afterward, we destroyed the spiritual graveyard with the power of God and great victory. Amen!

Since that day, the number of churches in that city is multiplying. Today, El Rey Jesús is one of the largest Hispanic churches in the United States.

We found the same design in the city of Cassadaga, near Orlando, Florida. As we prayed to deliver that city from the demonic influence that controlled it, we saw in the Spirit a cemetery with all the names of famous pastors from Orlando, including those that have already left the city. This town is known for the occult, and the devil sends a flow of satanic spells specifically over many of the Orlando amusement parks.

Among the tombs of the cemetery was a throne dedicated to satan. There is a flag of the United States surrounded by witchcraft, indicating the country's consecration to the devil. In the Spirit, God showed us a pastors' cemetery around the flag. They were buried there in order to kill them spiritually. There were churches and many pastors who had revival in Orlando's history, but had fallen into sin. There were others who moved to other states at the height of their growth.

We destroyed that place spiritually, and God has begun to do many wonderful things in Orlando.

The Region of Death

This is the dwelling place of those who have departed from this world. Sometimes in funeral homes or on accident scenes, the Lord leads us to ask Him for a resurrection. A dead person or someone whom you are trying to bring back to life must be removed from this region of death. Only God can grant resurrections. Life and death are His alone.

Once while preaching a message about resurrecting the dead in the city of Giradot in Colombia, a woman shouted in the middle of the service that a child had fallen from the fourth floor and had died. She begged us to go and try to resuscitate him. The pastors' enthusiasm encouraged me to go the funerary for the child.

We removed the people from the room and only those who had faith to see him raised from the dead remained. The Lord showed us a desolate region; it looked like a valley of trees and dried leaves. Among the withered leaves were forgotten graves. The Holy Spirit said *"You are seeing the region of death."*

The Lord asked me to open one of the tombs. The boy was inside a deep pit. I took him by the hands in order to pull him out. He was cold and stiff. A powerful force anchored him to that place. We cried with all our might for the power of the resurrection. The funerary room filled with the glory of God. A wave of life was forming, and we had no doubt the boy would rise from the dead. A shining throne appeared, covered in a white cloud. It was the Father. His clothes covered the small casket, and next to Him was Jesus. They talked to one another, but we could not hear anything. The moment was solemn. Then, I asked them to grant us this resurrection. Jesus looked at us and said He could not do it. He explained that the boy was with them, but if he returned, his soul would be lost.

Then they disappeared. We looked at one another with joy, satisfied with the Lord's decision.

Although the boy did not rise from the dead, something wonderful happened. The Father and Son descended in response to our prayer, and the spirit of death over the city was destroyed. In the days that followed, the power of resurrection touched everything. Dead churches were filled with life. Everything in the city received life.

God allowed the incident of the boy's death to bring resurrection to the city. Glory to His name!

Abaddon

Abaddon is the deepest part of the Abyss. I want to give it special treatment here because this is the place where the devil forges his plans of destruction.

> *They had as king over them the angel of the Abyss, whose name in Hebrew is Abaddon, and in Greek, Apollyon* (Revelation 9:11).

I have often wondered whether it is just a coincidence that the "address" of this verse is 9:11, the date the Twin Towers of New York were destroyed.

I remember an occasion when a powerful servant of God in the United States approached me. In a relatively short period of time, he had had a series of automobile accidents and felt that death was trying to harass him insistently. When I heard this man's testimony, the Holy Spirit immediately confirmed what I suspected: he was under the design of destruction and his soul had been taken captive in order to destroy his ministry at any cost. This design had been built in Abaddon (mash-shoo-aw). *Abaddon* comes from a Hebrew word having to do with destruction or "perishing."[5] Asaph refers to this place of perpetual desolation.

Lift up Your feet to the perpetual desolations. The enemy has damaged everything in the sanctuary....They said in their hearts, "Let us destroy them altogether." They have burned up all the meeting places of God in the land (Psalms 74:3,8 NKJV).

The devil destroys homes, lives, ministries, and entire cities from this sinister place. The murder of millions of babies is carried out. The designs of terrorism are forged from Abaddon. War, genocide, the shedding of innocent blood, as well as natural disasters, such as earthquakes and hurricanes, originate from this place.

The minister we prayed for was bound to a design of insatiable death. We were allowed to see this region. We saw in the Spirit a dark place at the bottom of the ocean. We knew we were penetrating the Abyss. A deeper region opened up below us after we arrived at the bottom of the waters.

A place was seen that looked like an enormous fortress made of black rocks with other places of labyrinths. There were huge demons inside ovens forging arms and weapons.

Among some destroyed automobiles, we found the minister we were searching for. He was bound in a car crash with a horrible demon guarding him. The angel accompanying us in the vision held a scroll the Father had given him. It was the certificate to set His servant free. The guard did not resist and we took the man from the place. To the best of my knowledge, he has been accident-free since.

It is interesting to observe that on earth he was suffering one accident after another while he was bound to the automobile in Abaddon. Nothing serious happened to him, because his life was in God's hands and not the devil's.

On another occasion, I had an experience that left me perplexed for a long time. Another servant of God in the United States approached me with severe financial problems. His father had been a military man and was in several wars. God does not call anyone to serve Him and then keep them in poverty. God is good and takes care of His servants.

I began to pray until God showed me the region where he was captive. He was in Abaddon. I did not see the same fortress I had seen before; this time it was a valley. A powerful angel appeared to lead me inside this vision.

I saw an enormous bloody plain with body parts strewn all around. The scene shocked me at first, but the presence of God's powerful messenger encouraged me. We walked for a while until we saw a gigantic demon. His image is still etched in my memory. He had enormous claws and growled thunderously. He was around 200 feet tall and would thrust his hands into a multitude of men clutching dozens of them at a time. Then he squeezed so hard they fell into pieces to the ground. This happened over and over again. He was between beast and man and was seated upon a mountain of incalculable riches.

The angel said this demon was *the Slaughterer.* (see figure on page 112) The United States sold their children for money in the Vietnam War: The war involved lots of money and many young Americans died. The angelic messenger said this gave the demon the right to destroy and steal the riches of a nation.

The angel instructed me to hide behind his wings. We stealthily approached, careful not to let the demon see us as we came to the opening between his parted legs. Once inside the mountain of riches, we made our way through a tunnel of gold. This led to the minister's father in a dungeon. The man was hugging an enormous treasure that he jealously guarded, but could not use because he was captive. Under the direction of the Holy Spirit, I told the man to ask forgiveness for having participated in the war. He humbly asked forgiveness and gave us his treasure. In the same cell was his son; we removed them from there and since that time he has prospered.

El Masacrador, *The Slaughterer*

Ananda Lamas Valle
anandalamas@gmail.com

One thing we must proclaim in Abaddon is that the truth—Jesus, the Son of God—has set us free. He set the captives free and announced the opening of prisons to those bound.

> *Shall Your lovingkindness be declared in the grave? Or Your faithfulness in the place of destruction?* (Psalms 88:11 NKJV)

Yes, it is!

The Place of Jackals

Abaddon has various regions and one is called "the place (or haunt) of jackals." In some translations, such as the King James Version, it is called the "place of dragons." It is a place in which the soul feels as if it is being attacked by wild beasts; the devourer mentioned in Malachi 3:11 (KJV) is one of them. He devours finances, health, projects, dreams, and everything else within his reach. It is a place of brokenness and great destruction and it is a place of God's judgment.

> *But you crushed us and made us a haunt for jackals and covered us over with deep darkness* (Psalms 44:19).

The Bible speaks about desolate and deserted cities full of jackals. In the spiritual sense, they are devouring demons destroying everything in one's life, whether the person is a servant of God or an unbeliever. In this passage, the sons of Korah cried out because they were being persecuted for the cause of the Most High.

The Roman Coliseum was a physical manifestation of this spiritual region. Lions devoured Christians because the emperors of ancient Rome received the inspiration of this design from hell. In fact, they reproduced it in every detail.

King David was harassed in his soul by these spiritual beasts. The soul feels as if it is being torn apart in this place of affliction.

I am in the midst of lions; I lie among ravenous beasts—
men whose teeth are spears and arrows, whose tongues
are sharp swords (Psalms 57:4).

An individual, city, or a nation under God's judgment, can be destroyed in this manner.

In Abaddon, people are held captive and literally devoured by these beasts. The Scripture says the devil roams about like a roaring lion, seeking whom he may devour (see 1 Pet. 5:8).

There are entire cities held in this region of wild beasts. The cities of *Nezahualcoyotl* (meaning "Place of Coyotes") and *Coatzacoalcos* (meaning "Place of Serpents [or Dragons]") are located in my country, Mexico. Both cities suffer the devastating impact of these spirits.

On one occasion, in the church I pastored in Mexico, we discovered sin among two of our leaders. Both had opened doors to spirits of sexual uncleanness.

The church experienced a period of spiritual death during that time. We brought the leadership together and sought the Spirit to discover what was happening. The church was in a pit at the bottom of a series of tunnels. Rats and jackals were everywhere.

Angels sent to help us led us through the passages. One by one, we began to find the brothers of the congregation. The rodents had bitten them. We took them out of that spiritual atmosphere one at a time. When we finished, the entire church was delivered and lifted to heavenly places. During the next Sunday's service, we witnessed the difference. The church was again full of the Holy Spirit.

The Land of Forgetfulness

Shall Your wonders be known in the dark? And Your
righteousness in the land of forgetfulness? (Psalms 88:12
NKJV)

This is a place of infinite loneliness, sadness, abandonment, and rejection. It is a place where the devil imprisons people in order for them to live their lives forgotten by others. After their names are placed in the land of forgetfulness, no one remembers them.

A man in a church approached me one time, asking me for help. His face was very sad and I felt the compassion to help him. I asked him what his problem was and he answered that he lived in terrible loneliness; he felt as though he didn't exist.

"No one ever remembers my name," he said. "I have gone to the same church for years and no one knows me. They continually ask me for my name."

"What is your name?" I asked.

I expected to hear him say an unpronounceable name, perhaps one that was a Greek or Russian name. Instead, he answered, "My name is William." It seemed strange that no one could remember such a common name.

He continued by saying, "When preachers make altar calls, they pray for everyone, but skip me. It is as though they can't see me. I sign up to serve in some way for the church, but it is as though my name were erased from the list. No one ever calls me."

I entered the Spirit, looking for direction, when a beautiful angel appeared and told me to follow him. Suddenly, everything disappeared and I could only see the angel and the light that came from his body shining over me. Around us was what appeared to be a concrete wall and walking was like entering into clouds. I asked where we were because I couldn't see anything clearly.

The angel responded, "We are in the land of forgetfulness. Here, everything disappears and is forgotten. That is why you can't see anything."

I followed the angel closely so I wouldn't get lost. As we walked, I began to make out very vaguely some bubbles inside the concrete-like structure we were in. It was like being inside of Swiss cheese.

William's Ancestor watching over his generations captivity.

Ananda Lamas Valle
anandalamas@gmail.com

Inside the solid bubbles, there were people in solitary confinement. Soon, we arrived at one of these holes and found an old man sitting in front of a trunk. The angel instructed me to order the old man to open the chest. He told me the man was William's ancestor, who made a covenant to lock his future generations in the chest.

I ordered him to allow his descendants to come out. He opened the lid and before my confused eyes, I saw a series of people leave. William and his two sons were among them. We took them out of the land of forgetfulness. I noticed a distinct glow to William's eyes after the vision. His countenance had changed. Two years later, I returned to find him busy in the church. Everyone loved him and remembered him with great affection.

I want to be clear that I was not invoking the dead when I saw William's ancestor. I was interacting in a vision in the spiritual realm. In other words, I was seeing a vision of something that happened, not in the natural realm, but in the spiritual. It is like having a dream in which one sees someone who has already died. I was not invoking the dead; I was in the realm of visions and revelations.

God Puts People in Prisons, Too

Another important thing to understand is this: Not only do traumas and difficult circumstances take us to regions of captivity, but God Himself can put us there.

Those who sat in darkness and in the shadow of death, Bound in affliction and irons—because they rebelled against the words of God, and despised the counsel of the Most High, therefore He brought down their heart with labor; they fell down, and there was none to help. Then they cried out to the Lord in their trouble, and He saved them out of their distresses. He brought them out of darkness and the shadow of death, and broke their chains in pieces. Oh, that men would give thanks to the Lord for His goodness, and for His wonderful works to the children of men! For He has broken the gates of bronze, and cut the bars of iron in two. Fools, because of their transgression, and because of their iniquities, were afflicted. Their soul abhorred all manner of food, and they drew near to the gates of death. Then they cried out to the Lord in their trouble, and He saved them out of their distresses. He sent His word and healed them, and delivered them from their destructions (Psalms 107:10-20 NKJV).

How many people are in this condition in the Church today because they choose their own paths and despised the Word and counsel of Jehovah? And how many leaders are suffering from sicknesses and tremendous pain because of their religiosity? God desires to take them in some direction, but because they are bound to their own systems and doctrines, they refuse to change.

Simply put, controlling our own lives and not glorifying God for everything can lead us to these regions.

Give glory to the Lord your God before He brings the darkness, before your feet stumble on the darkening hills. You hope for light, but He will turn it to thick darkness and change it to deep gloom. But if you do not listen, I will weep in secret because of your pride; my eyes will weep bitterly, overflowing with tears, because the Lord's flock will be taken captive (Jeremiah 13:16-17).

Bitter people who cannot forgive end up in these prisons. Jesus taught about the servant whose lord had forgiven him a great debt but he refused to forgive the one who was indebted to him.

In anger his master turned him over to the jailers...until he should pay back all he owed. This is how my heavenly

Father will treat each of you unless you forgive your brother from your heart (Matthew 18:34-35).

Before we proceed, it is important for us to take stock of our own spiritual condition. We must allow God to reveal any areas of imprisonment, so that we can strip off the shackles, be free, and set others free.

ENDNOTES

1. John Sandford and Paula Sandford, *Healing the Wounded Spirit* (Tulsa, OK: Victory House Publishers, 1985), 149-150.

2. *Biblesoft's New Exhaustive Strong's Numbers and Concordance with Expanded Greek-Hebrew Dictionary.* CD-ROM. Biblesoft, Inc. and International Bible Translators, Inc. s.v. "she'owl," (OT 7585).

3. 4758. hRa√rAm mar}eh, *mar-eh´*; from 7200; a view (the act of seeing); also an appearance (the thing seen), whether (real) a shape (especially if handsome, comeliness; often plural the looks), or (mental) a vision:—apparently, appearance(-reth), as soon as beautiful(-ly), countenance, fair, favored, form, goodly, to look (up) on (to), look(-eth), pattern, to see, seem, sight, visage, vision.

    8544. hÎn...wm;Vt tmuwnah, *tem-oo-naw´*; or hÎnUm;Vt tmunah, *tem-oo-naw´*; from 4327; something portioned (i.e. fashioned) out, as a shape, i.e., (indefinitely) phantom, or (specifically) embodiment, or (figuratively) manifestation (of favor)—image, likeness, similitude.

4. *Biblesoft's New Exhaustive Strong's Numbers and Concordance with Expanded Greek-Hebrew Dictionary.* CD-ROM. Biblesoft, Inc. and International Bible Translators, Inc. s.v. "*tmuwnah*," 8544 from 4327.

5. *Biblesoft's New Exhaustive Strong's Numbers and Concordance with Expanded Greek-Hebrew Dictionary.* CD-ROM. Biblesoft, Inc. and International Bible Translators, Inc. s.v. "abaddown," (OT 11).

Chapter 7

Setting the Captives Free

Setting the captives free is part of our calling. God wants all believers to heal the sick, cast out demons, raise the dead, and set the
captives free.

Once, when the disciples could not cast out a demon, Jesus told
them that the particular type of demon would come out only by prayer
and fasting (see Matt. 17:21). How should we pray? What type of fasting
should we do?

> *Is not this the kind of fasting I have chosen: to loose the*
> *chains of injustice and untie the cords of the yoke, **to set***
> ***the oppressed free** and break every yoke?* (Isaiah 58:6)

In the original Hebrew, the word rendered "oppressed" refers to
those whose souls are torn apart.[1] In this passage, we find a full range of
deliverances from yokes of the devil to bands of iniquity.[2]

Fasting is a practice that sensitizes us to the spiritual world so that we
can hear and see the Kingdom of God. It assists us in praying effectively
under a prophetic anointing to deliver persons being held captive.

Fasting has many purposes. It is not simply a religious act to battle
our flesh. It covers those who dwell in Him with the power of God so we
can love as Jesus loved. His love is full of compassion.

When we see souls tormented by the devil, what kind of Christianity must we offer? It is the true love of Jesus, which leads us to give our lives to find answers from the depths of God. His ways are higher than our ways and the natural mind cannot understand them.

Jesus' Bride goes wherever He goes. She is not afraid because perfect love casts out fear. She trusts Him, even if it means experiencing the darkest places on earth to rescue a soul from the flames of hell. Setting the captives free is the call of God's love to those who love Him more than they love themselves.

We have studied the places of captivity of the soul. Now we are going to learn a form of deliverance that is much easier than the traditional way of casting out demons.

The fragmented soul is ministered to from the captive place where it is found. The captive soul will see, hear, and feel everything that is happening in the place of its imprisonment. If it is taken to heavenly places, it will hear and feel everything happening in Heaven and will enjoy all of its benefits.

> *And God raised us up with Christ and seated us with Him in the heavenly realms in Christ Jesus, in order that in the coming ages He might show the incomparable riches of his grace, expressed in His kindness to us in Christ Jesus* (Ephesians 2:6-7).

Jesus took our captivity and seated us with Him in heavenly places. Unfortunately, this does not happen automatically after we say, "Lord, Lord, come and live in my heart." Everything Jesus did gives us legal right to it. In other words, Jesus signed the check, but we must cash it. *Most people in the Church today save the check for when they die, never enjoying the abundant life on earth that Jesus purchased for them.* God wants us to possess all the riches of His grace right now.

Jesus died for the sins of the world, but this doesn't automatically save the earth. *Each of us must receive the Gospel, repent from our sins, leave our vain ways of living, invite Jesus in our hearts, and truly make Him the Lord of our lives. Only then are we saved.*

The same thing happens when we say He took our captivity captive and seated us in heavenly places. He gave us the victory so we can leave our captivity without opposition. He opened the way for each part of the soul to be established in heavenly places with Him.

> *In an acceptable time I have heard You, and in the day of salvation I have helped You; I will preserve You and give You as a covenant to the people, to restore the earth, to cause them to inherit the desolate heritages; that You may say to the prisoners, "Go forth," to those who are in darkness, "Show yourselves." They shall feed along the roads, and their pastures shall be on all desolate heights. They shall neither hunger nor thirst, neither heat nor sun shall strike them; for He who has mercy on them will lead them, even by the springs of water He will guide them* (Isaiah 49:8-10 NKJV).

In this passage, God has sent us to set the captives free and to restore the earth; *to call the prisoners to come out and to tell those who are in darkness to show themselves.* Once that is done, they need only to be established in Heaven, where they can eat and drink of God in the pastures on the hills next to springs of water.

We must understand the basics. Each part of the soul must be established in heavenly places: our character, our will, our emotions, the sexual areas, our thoughts, and every captive fragment. We must surrender our souls to Jesus and be ministered to from Heaven, piece by piece.

The process of setting a person free from captivity is simpler than delivering someone who is demon-possessed. Why is this true?

If we truly are in Him, we hold the keys of death and hell and are full of the Holy Spirit. The invisible Kingdom of God manifests through the prophetic anointing making us one with Him. If our understanding interferes with our spirit and we try to cast out demons in the traditional way, we will not obtain the desired result because of doubt and unbelief. Doing things the prophetic way is much simpler and requires less effort, as will be described later.

Everything Jesus did on earth was totally dependent on the prophetic Holy Spirit anointing.

> *Jesus gave them this answer: "I tell you the truth, the Son can do nothing by Himself; He can do only what He sees His Father doing, because* **whatever the Father does the Son also does.** *For the Father loves the Son and shows Him all He does. Yes, to your amazement He will show Him even greater things than these* (John 5:19-20).

Every healing, miracle, or deliverance was done in the spiritual world. Jesus spent time praying, seeking the Father's direction in the Spirit.

Jesus did not let his friend Lazarus die (see John 11). The Father showed Him in a vision Lazarus leaving the region of the dead and rising from the dead. The same visible and audible reality of the Kingdom of God through the prophetic anointing of the Holy Spirit is the heritage He left us.

I have my own theory about what happened when Jesus went to deliver the demon-possessed man from the country of the Gadarene (see Luke 8:26-36; Mark 5:1-13). This was the region of the shadow of death, in the land of Nephtali and Zebulun, which Isaiah prophesied:

> *...at first He lightly esteemed the land of Zebulun and the land of Naphtali, and afterward more heavily oppressed her, by the way of the sea, beyond the Jordan, in Galilee of the Gentiles. The people who walked in darkness have seen a great light;* **those who dwelt in the land of the shadow of death,** *upon them a light has shined* (Isaiah 9:1-2 NKJV).

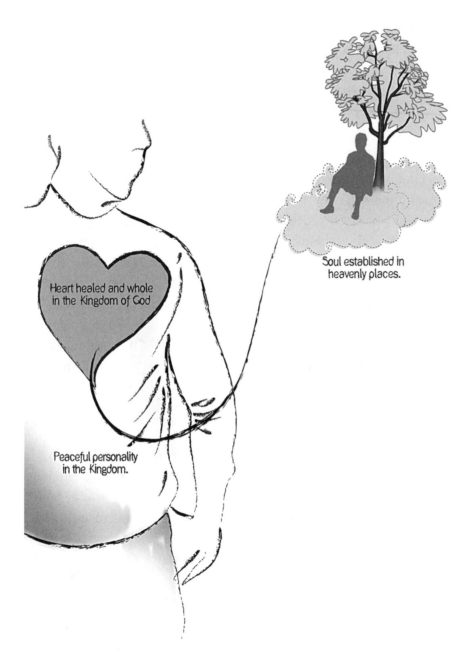

Soul established in
heavenly places.

Heart healed and whole
in the Kingdom of God

Peaceful personality
in the Kingdom.

Figure 3

Ananda Lamas Valle
anandalamas@gmail.com

The reason Jesus went there, on the Sea of Galilee, was to set the man free. That liberation affected the entire region. I believe the principality of the area was the demon called *Legion* who possessed the man from Gadarene. The young man dwelt in the cemetery where the deliverance occurred. The graveyards are gates of hell and a good place for a territorial power to have its headquarters. Jesus arrived with a purpose. He knew He was going there to fight against a territorial spirit.

On their way there, Jesus and the disciples encountered a storm that arose on the water (see Luke 8:20-25). As the storm raged, the disciples found Jesus asleep in the boat. If I were about to face a principality in the regions of death, I would choose to pray and not sleep. So why did Jesus sleep? Some trances or visions in the Bible happened while the servant of God entered into a deep sleep. This is what happened in the case of Daniel. The people of Israel were at that time captives in Babylon and he prayed and fasted until the angel of the Lord manifested unto him. He fell into a deep sleep and there he saw the Angel of the Lord that came to help him. During this trance he saw Michael, Prince of the hosts of heaven fighting against the King of Persia in the spiritual realm. That battle lead to the deliverance of Israel from their captivity (see Daniel 10:8-13).

I believe Jesus was in a trance in which He fell into a deep sleep and there fought against the demon, Legion of Gadarene. I have fought huge battles while sleeping. My body was in bed, but my spirit was in action. While Jesus was in the boat, the battle in the Spirit unleashed the physical manifestation of a storm. I have seen this climatological reaction many times when we are setting a city free and entering the spiritual world. When Jesus was awakened by His disciples, He rebuked the wind and the raging of the water, which is how you deal with the spirit of darkness.

When the storm was over, Jesus had won the battle in the Spirit against Legion and delivered the soul of the man from the regions of Sheol. This was why the demon-possessed man ran to meet Him and kneel before Him.

*When he saw Jesus from a distance, he ran and fell on his
knees in front of Him* (Mark 5:6).

His soul had been set free for him to do this although the unclean
spirit still lived within him. It was through this victim that the entire
region was controlled.

And he [Legion] *begged Jesus again and again not to send
them out of the area* (Mark 5:10).

This is how territorial spirits talk. The territory is more important
to them than human beings. We have witnessed this kind of thing many
times after liberating cities and territories. Storms are present when
entering the prophetic dimensions and waging war in the Spirit. Afterward, wonderful deliverances occur in the people who were tormented
by the devil.

Traditional deliverance concentrates on casting out demons from the
person, but leaves the person in prison. That soul will feel partial relief
because its tormentors have been cast out. Nevertheless, the individual
will not enter the levels of glory and freedom from sitting in heavenly
places with Jesus because imprisonment continues. New tormentors will
be sent. Traditional liberators will think the demons returned because
the person opened a door of some kind, but the reality is the person was
never truly set free in the first place.

Prophetic deliverance sets the captive free from prison without having to deal with the demons. If one is present at the moment of the deliverance, we may have to deal with a demon guard; but in most cases, the
cells are not guarded. This makes the rescue easier.

Once the person is outside and established in heavenly places, the
demons that tormented that soul are no longer around. The results of
this type of deliverance are much more powerful and easier to carry out.
Only rarely do you deal with demons inside the person after a deliverance from captivity.

THE PROCESS OF DELIVERANCE FROM CAPTIVITY

Not everyone is gifted prophetically to see the Kingdom of God and the kingdom of darkness. This is primarily because of erroneous teaching. The truth is anyone who has the Holy Spirit can enter the prophetic dimensions necessary to achieve deliverances. The Holy Spirit is *inherently* prophetic. Therefore, there is no such thing as having the Holy Spirit and not being able to have these manifestations.

> *In the last days, God says, I will pour out My Spirit on all people. Your sons and daughters will **prophesy**, your young men will see **visions**, your old men will dream dreams. Even on My servants, both men and women, I will pour out My Spirit in those days, and they will **prophesy*** (Acts 2:17-18).

See? Everyone who is Spirit-filled has the prophetic anointing. So, if you have the Spirit of God, believe it and develop this ability.

By Faith and Declaring the Word

The captivity of a person is discovered by listening to that individual. Allow the Holy Spirit through the word of knowledge and prophecy to show you the specific region of captivity.

If you are unable to see the spiritual world, do the deliverance by faith. Simply apply the truth established in Isaiah 49, *to* say to the captives, "Come out," and to those in darkness, "Show yourselves!" (see Isa. 49:9).

When ministering deliverance, I talk to people about their captivity and fill them with faith so that they believe God will set them free right away. For example, I ask the person to sit in a chair and close his or her eyes. I ask the person to feel the place of imprisonment. I concentrate in the Spirit and say, "I am standing in front of the prison where you are trapped, and I am opening the door." Then, I take the person by the hands and raise him or her from the chair, as if we were leaving that place. By talking through the process, I make sure the person feels that we are leaving.

Sometimes, captive souls are afraid to leave or fearful the devil will do something to them. If so, you must calm them down. With a warm, gentle voice, I encourage them and hug them. Once calm, we continue the process of walking out. People sometimes lose their composure and begin to experience terror. Command them to take control of the situation. Remind them they are in complete control of their own will and the devil has no power over their free will. Be firm and don't play the devil's game.

Once the person has regained the desire to leave, I resume the action of our leaving the place of captivity. We walk together and I explain that we are leaving together. After taking some steps I declare, "We are entering the regions of light."

> *I will lead the blind by ways they have not known, along unfamiliar paths I will guide them; I will turn the darkness into light before them and make the rough places smooth. These are the things I will do; I will not forsake them* (Isaiah 42:16).

I make sure they see the light and once they do I establish them in heavenly places. Remember, we can see and experience Heaven and earth in Jesus. The Kingdom of God makes Heaven accessible.

> *They will feed beside the roads and find pasture on every barren hill* (Isaiah 49:9b).

At other times, I lead them next to peaceful waters.

> *He who has compassion on them will guide them and lead them beside springs of water* (Isaiah 49:10b).

Sometimes I put them in Jesus' lap, in green pastures, or right next to the tree of life.

Then the angel showed me the river of the water of life, as clear as crystal, flowing from the throne of God and of the Lamb down the middle of the great street of the city. On each side of the river stood the tree of life, bearing twelve crops of fruit, yielding its fruit every month. And the leaves of the tree are for the healing of the nations (Revelation 22:1-2).

There are beautiful places there, dwellings of peace and security where the soul will never feel anguish or torment again.

My people will live in peaceful dwelling places, in secure homes, in undisturbed places of rest (Isaiah 32:18).

The places of light and knowledge are spiritual regions full of the presence and knowledge of God.

What is the way to the abode of light? And where does darkness reside? Can you take them to their places? Do you know the paths to their dwellings? (Job 38:19-20)

People set free from captivity will become increasingly hungry to experience the heavenly places. The Lord will guide you to the places in which to establish the people.

It is important to close the door of captivity. Declare the place forever closed to that person. Once the soul is established in Heaven, it will be ministered to by Heaven. It will experience peace like never before. Health will be restored and fears of torment will be gone.

Sometimes you must set the same person free from different places. But the most important thing is to teach them to depend on God, not you. Fill them with faith and the knowledge of Jesus. Believe in your authority in Christ and do not allow fear or unbelief to speak.

Prophetic Deliverance From Regions of Captivity

In the prophetic realm, our weapons are very powerful. All demons fear us and we have total authority. In reality, it is a very simple battle. Yet, we must be mature and full of understanding to enter this level of battle. Submission to the direction of the Holy Spirit, who directs the angels, is essential. As Jesus said, "I don't do anything that I don't see the Father doing" (see John 5:19). In this spiritual dimension, there are demons we are not allowed to touch. There are captives outside of our specific mission that we are not permitted to set free in a particular moment.

My advice to you who are not experienced in deliverance is to enter this level only after God releases you to do so. If your life is not in order or you do not have spiritual covering, wait until these factors are present. Always operate at the level of faith and authority Jesus has given you.

Once He has released you, the first thing to do is enter in the Spirit. That means to enter into deep worship where the noise of your mind is silenced. After the presence of God commands your attention, your eyes will be opened to see His Kingdom.

Normally, what manifests is the throne of God or His Court of Justice. Through the prophetic anointing, you can stand before the Lord's throne. Next, ask for authorization and angels to accompany you to rescue captives. When the angel or angels have been assigned to you, ask God for armor and weapons. Sometimes angels are awarded safe passage or keys that will be needed during the deliverance.

The Spirit will show you the spiritual world. The revelation gifts of knowledge and prophecy operate to demonstrate the Holy Spirit's authority in the matter.

From this position, our point of departure is this: He who is one with Jesus, is one Spirit with Him (see 1 Cor. 6:17). Also, in Jesus the heavens and the earth are one (see Eph. 1:10). So, if I am one Spirit with Jesus and the heavens are in Jesus, I have the possibility of seeing, hearing, and feeling everything that Jesus sees, hears, and feels in the Kingdom of Heaven. This premise is what I mean by entering the Kingdom of God.

As I said before, in the spiritual world we are 100 percent united in Spirit with Jesus; no doubt or flesh can interfere with that. It is like seeing a movie and then walking inside of it. You become like a subjective camera that takes the place of an actor in the movie and you see where the actor is going as if through his eyes.

Self-Deliverance From Captivity

Everyone who is full of the Holy Spirit can free himself. The most important part of your being, which is your spirit, has to be completely consecrated to Jesus. The Lord has given you all His authority; the keys of the Kingdom of God are for those who have the revelation of the Messiah in their hearts.

Among the keys of the Kingdom are those that unlock the regions of captivity.

> *And I also say to you that you are Peter, and on this rock I will build My church, and the gates of Hades shall not prevail against it. And I will give you the keys of the kingdom of heaven, and whatever you bind on earth will be bound in heaven, and whatever you loose on earth will be loosed in heaven* (Matthew 16:18-19 NKJV).

> *This is what the Lord says to His anointed, to Cyrus, whose right hand I take hold of to subdue nations before him and to strip kings of their armor,* **to open doors before him so that gates will not be shut: I will go before you and will level the mountains; I will break down gates of bronze and cut through bars of iron.** *I will give you the treasures of darkness, riches stored in secret places, so that you may know that I am the Lord, the God of Israel, who summons you by name* (Isaiah 45:1-3).

The same thing God told Cyrus, King of Persia, He is saying to all who have entered His Kingdom. Jesus has made us kings and priests, cleansed us, and given us a new name for God, His Father. Therefore, ask the Lord to show you the place of your captivity.

See yourself trapped, even if by a piece of your soul. See yourself opening the door of your captivity and setting yourself free. Cast out any demon opposing you. Do it by faith, believing Jesus is more powerful than any demon you may have.

Once the door of your captivity is open, break the shackles if there are any; take yourself by the hand out of there. Ask God to receive you in heavenly places and give Him that part of yourself. Anyone can do it. In Jesus, we are strong and powerful.

If you have the Holy Spirit, depend on Him and not people. The Spirit wants to train you and raise you up. He wants to make you a true son of God:

> because those **who are led by the Spirit of God are sons of God.** *For you did not receive a spirit that makes you a slave again to fear, but you received the Spirit of sonship. And by Him we cry, "Abba, Father"* (Romans 8:14-15).

I have taken this revelation very seriously in my life. I began establishing every piece of my soul in heavenly places. The parts that were in regions of death, I established them in places of health. I know that sickness cannot touch me. It can attack me, but it cannot prosper in my life. The parts that were in anguish, oppression, or fear, are now in places of peace, drinking from the springs of life. The parts that were harassed and brokenhearted by persecution are now in a fortified castle.

> *You shall hide them in the secret place of Your presence from the plots of man; You shall keep them secretly in a pavilion from the strife of tongues. Blessed be the Lord, for*

He has shown me His marvelous kindness in a strong city!
(Psalms 31:20-21 NKJV)

These are not just beautiful words. Jesus came to unite the heavens and the earth. This is what it means to possess His Kingdom. It causes His designs and benefits of Heaven to be manifested in our lives. But whether or not this occurs will depend upon the location of our souls.

Delivering Those Who Don't Want to Be Delivered

In certain cases, God can allow you to set someone free from captivity even if the person is not physically close to you or does not want to be delivered.

Many people don't want to be set free because their minds and hearts are in captivity. The Bible says:

*Teach us what we shall say unto him; for we cannot order our speech by reason of **darkness*** (Job 37:19 KJV).

The truth is, not that they don't want to be set free, but that darkness is hindering them from thinking properly.

In the story we talked about previously, when Jesus delivered the Gadarene, He first dealt with his spiritual captivity and he addressed physical person.

You can pray that the Lord will send angels to open the prisons of your beloved one, and command with authority that the gates of his or her prison are opening. Then call the person to come out, and to show him or herself into the light.

If this is the case of someone living with you, pray at night while they are sleeping and release the Holy Ghost over them to convict them of sin, and their need for Jesus.

If you are skillful in the prophetic and word of knowledge gifts, then ask the Lord to show you where the person is captive and pull him or her out of that prison.

Setting the Captives Free

This prayer will bring your beloved to want to be delivered or saved; at that point you can pray with them with their full agreement.

Recognize Your Source

In previous chapters, I talked about regions of death such as hospitals. These spiritual gates trap souls. We are used to hearing about God's children going to these places, and we have not stopped to consider that these places are not for us. Jesus did not pay such a horrible price, having been tortured and pierced for our sicknesses, so that we would then go to the hospital. That would be like Him saying, "I took away your sicknesses, but it really didn't work. So perhaps it would be best if you take medications made by men, because I have decided to use doctors. My stripes were not enough to get the job done." Isn't this the most ridiculous thing you have ever heard? Either He suffered for our sicknesses or He didn't! And if He did, why would it be the Father's will to ignore His Son's suffering and use the strength of man? Do you really believe that an antibiotic has more strength than the stripes of Jesus?

The very power that conquered sickness and death flows through those wounds. The problem is that our minds are trapped in regions of the fear of death. We want to have control over our health and not give it to God.

Medicine and hospitals killed my twin sister, my mother, and many of my friends. According to statistics 700,000 Americans die per year because of side effects of medications and a third of all people admitted to hospitals are there because of negative effects of medication.[3] But that will not be my destiny or that of those who want to go to greater heights with Jesus.

My husband and I made a covenant with God. We will not bow to Pharmakeia. This is the name that both the spirit of witchcraft and medicine go by. We said the same thing that Shadrach, Meshach, and Abednego said as they stood before the fiery furnace into which Nebuchadnezzar threatened to throw them:

135

If we are thrown into the blazing furnace, the God we serve is able to save us from it, and He will rescue us from your hand, O king. But even if He does not, we want you to know, O king, that we will not serve your gods or worship the image of gold you have set up (Daniel 3:17-18).

God is powerful enough to set us free from sickness! The stripes of Jesus were not in vain. If they are real, let them be real. If He chooses not to set us free, may He receive us into glory; but we will not bow.

Since we made this decree, sickness does not prosper in our home. Pain and the devil have no place in any form. We established our souls in places of health. We eat from the tree of life by taking Communion daily, and Jesus' stripes shine with power throughout our bodies. The Lord led us to exchange one organ at a time in our body, for Jesus' organs, heart, kidneys, lungs—*everything.*

Hospitals and medicine are for those who do not know Jesus and for those in the process of breaking through patterns or for those who don't know that they can live in this level of glory because they have not been taught about it. But God is calling you to greater levels in your relationship with Him. He wants you to reach radical victories because that is what Jesus conquered for you.

We do not condemn anyone in any way who still takes medicine or who needs surgery, but we want to announce to you that there are better and more lasting solutions that can be yours.

The soul must be established in God. We must learn to dwell in Him and with Him. We must make Heaven a reality that everyone can see in our lives. The soul that has been rescued and translated to regions of light is the one that dwells with the Lord and is nurtured by Him and evil cannot touch him.

God's dwelling is a place to be inhabited, not a place we visit on Sundays. It is the place of our peace and security.

He who dwells in the secret place of the Most High shall abide under the shadow of the Almighty. I will say of the Lord, "He is my refuge and my fortress; My God, in Him I will trust." Surely He shall deliver you from the snare of the fowler and from the perilous pestilence. He shall cover you with His feathers, and under His wings you shall take refuge; His truth shall be your shield and buckler. You shall not be afraid of the terror by night, nor of the arrow that flies by day, nor of the pestilence that walks in darkness, nor of the destruction that lays waste at noonday. A thousand may fall at your side, and ten thousand at your right hand; but it shall not come near you. Only with your eyes shall you look, and see the reward of the wicked. Because you have made the Lord, who is my refuge, even the Most High, your dwelling place, no evil shall befall you, nor shall any plague come near your dwelling; for He shall give His angels charge over you, to keep you in all your ways. In their hands they shall bear you up, lest you dash your foot against a stone. You shall tread upon the lion and the cobra, the young lion and the serpent you shall trample underfoot. "Because he has set his love upon Me, therefore I will deliver him; I will set him on high, because he has known My name. He shall call upon Me, and I will answer him; I will be with him in trouble; I will deliver him and honor him. With long life I will satisfy him, and show him My salvation" (Psalms 91:1-16 NKJV).

My desire is for this book to be an inspiration that challenges you to enter glorious liberty. My prayer is that it opens your vision and understanding to believe that you can live a life of peace, joy, and health in the Kingdom of God.

Take time for yourself, pinpoint the areas of your life in which you do not experience the total victory that Jesus bought for you with His blood. Ask the Holy Spirit to show you where your soul might be held captive.

Then take the authority Jesus gave you and make up your mind to be set free.

Remember, your will is yours and no one else's. God cannot touch it, the devil even less so. Then, make up your mind to be free, no matter what the cost, and you will see how the devil will flee from your life.

> *I can do everything through Him who gives me strength* (Philippians 4:13).

Listen to the call of God, first to be set free and then to free others.

> *I, the Lord, have called you in righteousness; I will take hold of your hand. I will keep you and will make you to be a covenant for the people and a light for the Gentiles, to open eyes that are blind, to free captives from prison and to release from the dungeon those who sit in darkness* (Isaiah 42:6-7).

The offer of complete freedom in Christ still stands. Our Savior has paid handsomely for it. It is up to us to enter in to the depths of salvation and help others to join us there. It is a kind of freedom that has been experienced all around the world, as you are about to see.

ENDNOTES

1. 7533. XAxǝr ratsats, *raw-tsats*'; a primitive root; to crack in pieces, literally or figuratively:—break, bruise, crush, discourage, oppress, struggle together.

2. Biblesoft's New Exhaustive *Strong's* Numbers and Concordance with Expanded Greek-Hebrew Dictionary. CD-ROM. Biblesoft, Inc. and International Bible Translators, Inc.; 2784. h;DbUx√rAj chartsubbah, *khar-tsoob-baw*'; of uncertain derivation; a fetter; figuratively, a pain:—band; 7562. oÅv°rresha{, *reh'-shah;* from 7561; a wrong (especially moral):—iniquity, wicked(-ness); 4133. hDfwøm mowtah, *mo-taw*'; feminine of 4132; a pole; by implication, an ox-bow; hence, a yoke (either literal or figurative):—bands, heavy, staves, yoke.

3.   Guylaine Lanctot, *The Medical Mafia: How to Get Out Alive and Take Back Our Health and Wealth* (Here's the Key Inc., 1995), 32.

Section Two

Amazing Testimonies of Deliverance From Captivity

Chapter 8

A Gadarene
by Prophetess Flory González

MÉXICO

The Powerful Deliverance of
a Satanist Living in a Cave in Brazil

My name is Flory Gonzales, I have a prophetic ministry in Mexico City and have been part of Dr. Ana Mendez Ferrell's spiritual warfare team for more than 20 years.

In 2005 a group of Brazilean intercessors and I went into spiritual warfare around Rio de Janeiro, Brazil's capital city, in order to set it free. The night before we left for the city of Petropolis, the Lord gave me a dream. I saw myself entering a cave. It was full of demons. I saw witches and witchdoctors making all kinds of covenants over the region. The Lord showed me what looked like the headquarters from which the enemy operated to bind in covenant thousands of people to himself. When I woke up, I knew in my spirit that the place in my dream was real and that we had to find it.

I began to ask the pastors and intercessors on our team if they knew about such a place, but no one did. However, God orchestrated everything.

We began our journey and supernaturally, the Lord made me stop the car on a dirt road. My heart beat rapidly as the Lord clearly commanded me to take a certain path. So we did. Soon after that, we discovered the place I had seen in my dreams.

We got out of the truck, excited to see the precision with which the Lord directed us. Hanging from the trees and stuck into the nooks around the cave were all kinds of works of witchcraft. There were photographs, locks of hair tied with red and black cords, empty containers, burned rocks, and remainders of wax. A smell of decay and death permeated the place.

As we got closer, the odor of decomposing blood nauseated us. We covered our faces to enter the cave. Everywhere there were *knisis.* These are jars where works of voodoo and the *Umbanda* (a type of high magic) are kept to attract evil spirits.

In my heart, I asked God what to do. How were we going to cancel all those spells? But He said to me, *"I didn't bring you here for that. I want you to go to the back of the cave."* I was a little surprised by His response, but I obeyed.

We advanced slowly. It was literally like entering hell. It smelled like rotten flesh; the odor made the way almost unbearable. Upon reaching the deepest part in the darkness, illuminated by spell candles, we could barely make out a being that peered at us. It was a very thin and dirty young man.

His beard and long fingernails were full of dried blood and excrement. His face and his clothing were covered by a thick crust. He lay curled up beside an extinguished fire in which you could still smell burnt flesh and the herbs of spells. Hanging from his neck were colorful, beaded voodoo necklaces used for protection. His presence was dark and evil.

Suddenly, his eyes locked onto mine. I was looking at the devil in flesh and blood. With a dry, mocking voice he asked us if we, too, had come to bury the living. "No," I exclaimed with great authority. "We came for you." He began to laugh, scoffing at us. In my spirit, I prayed the whole time, seeking God's direction. I was calm and in total control. The voice of the Lord told me to take him out of there to the entrance of the cave. I knew this was like the case of the demon-possessed man who lived among the tombs in the country of the Gadarene—the man whom Jesus delivered (see Mark 5; Luke 8).

The presence of God strengthened me, filling me with courage. Without hesitation, I took him by the hand. "You're burning me! You're burning me!" he screamed as he allowed me to guide him to the entrance of the cave. I knew that there were angels guarding us the whole time.

I heard Jesus' voice say, "He is a pastor's son." I froze. But with confidence I said, "Your father is a pastor. What are you doing here?"

The boy became filled with rage and at the same time, with pain. He declared that his father had raped him and had given him to a *babalao* (a Brazilian witchdoctor) when he was six years old. The babalao had trained the boy to do all kinds of witchcraft, turn people into zombies, and carry out the greatest spells through Umbanda and Comdomble (another type of high magic).

Then his voice changed and with malice, he asked my name. I did not tell him what it was. The warriors prayed without ceasing, some inside and some outside of the cave. You could feel the oppression and the tension of a fierce battle.

I silently took authority and began to worship God while I entered the Spirit realm. The Lord prompted me to set him free from his captivities. That cave was a physical manifestation of the terrible prisons in which he was living.

A vision opened before me and I saw myself before the throne of God. His presence covered me with an armor made of a mixture of gold and light. An enormous angel came to meet me. He held in his hands a sword and shield. The Lord instructed me to follow him. We began to enter deep places. They were like caverns that led to even greater depths. You could hear the screams of tormented people, but the Lord did not allow me to look at them. He urged me to worship Him continually in my spirit and not to turn around, no matter what I heard.

We came to a place where there were many small caverns closed off with iron bars and guarded by demons. Each cavern corresponded to the type of torment being inflicted there. The fragmented soul of the young man was found trapped in every one of them. At the entrance, there was a gigantic, muscular guard who was a mix of man and beast.

The angel said, "His name is *Rape*. Ask the young man to forgive his father's sin, and you must order the demon to leave and to stop guarding these prisons." I did it. I took over the place, identifying myself as a child of God so that the Lord could receive my intercession. Then I commanded the demon to leave. He could not see me, as the light from my armor blinded him and greatly intimidated him. Suddenly, various angels appeared next to us; they wrapped the demon in a kind of net and took him away.

We continued walking and entered a cave of dense darkness. It was an indescribable blackness. We heard the screams and moans of someone in great pain. The light that radiated from us illuminated the scene. It was this young man; he was chained with shackles to the wall of a cave. Various demons tortured and mocked him. They said, "You will stay here forever. When you die you will come here." As they jabbed him with needles in his body and even in his eyes, they reminded him of all the spells of witchcraft he had carried out. It was both mental and physical punishment. I heard them say, "You gave us this right!" They yelled and laughed at him.

The boy's soul cried and cursed. They never stopped hurting him. We heard voodoo drums and the rhythms of chanting. For every drumbeat there was a crack of a whip.

I looked at the scene, asking the Holy Spirit what to do because there were many strong, terrible demons all around the young man. The Holy Spirit replied, "Be at peace. They fear you because they see My light. Simply tell them to get out because they no longer have anyone to protect them." The Lord revealed to me that, without the guard, they were completely vulnerable.

We opened the gate and were going to enter, but we realized there was no floor. There were seemingly bottomless holes through which the demon-tormentors came and went. Upon seeing us, they sank into the abysses, leaving the young man alone. The angel removed his shackles, at which point, I could see his face. He was a weak, tormented teenager.

A wonderful presence could be felt at that moment. Jesus had descended to that place. He shone with light and His love flooded everything. We saw how the boy's soul melted inside the Lord's body. As we left, the pits closed behind us.

We continued moving forward and Jesus went with us. We arrived at another cave. It wasn't as black as the earlier one. Still, hatred and unspeakable pain could be felt in the air. It was a prison of rape. Among all the dungeons, this was the one the main guardian kept with more zeal. We saw the fragment of the soul that we were seeking. It was the same young man, but he was only six years old. Demons raped him one after another as he cursed his parents. In spite of his young age, hatred and homicide were in his eyes. He cursed continuously and every time hatred left his mouth, the cave filled with the stench of death. A putrid liquid ran down the walls. It was bitterness.

Inside the cave, the moment in which his father had raped him replayed over and over as though it were a movie. We could see how brutally the father had beaten the boy as he robbed him of his innocence.

The boy screamed, full of hatred toward the image of his father. "I don't believe in God! I wish you were dead!"

I began to ask him to forgive me, as though I were his father. I was also crying, trying to convince him that Jesus loved him. I explained what had happened to him did not come from God. He yelled that the only one who loved him was satan. I began to cry out for mercy and to forgive as if I were the boy.

He cried, "Shut up! Shut up, you are hurting me." But as I forgave, the soul began to calm down. When he was tranquil, I again asked him to forgive me, as if I were his father. He accepted and we were able to take him out of there.

It was the same as it had been in the previous cave. We shone the light of Jesus and commanded the demons to leave. They were expelled upon seeing us. Then the soul of the little boy ran to Jesus and melted into Him.

Next, we arrived at a third cave, where we found another fragment of the young man's soul. The floor was made of mud and serpents crawled around it, biting him. They squirted hatred from their fangs and injected it into the young man's soul. At every bite, he cursed and swore without stopping. It was continual torment. The soul was covered in festering bites that oozed a smelly, disgusting venom. The boy's soul writhed in pain. Once more, upon seeing us, the serpents fled and we were free to take the young man from that place and reunite him with Jesus.

The last cave in which we found him was empty. There were no demons guarding him. Curled up like a frightened animal, the young man's soul cried bitterly. He was only a little boy. We approached him to take him out of there, but he didn't want to leave. He was very frightened. I told him that Jesus loved him and that He wanted to take him out of that place.

Sobbing, he told me that he didn't love Jesus. He said that it was a lie that Jesus loved him. "He doesn't love me! He doesn't love me!" he said, his words broken up with his crying. I told him that Jesus had sent me to help him.

The angel then took the boy into his arms. The boy curled up on the angel's shoulder and allowed the angel to carry him out of that cave. Upon leaving, he turned into a small baby and was united with Jesus.

I understood that rejection had imprisoned him from the time he had been in his mother's womb.

The Lord ordered me to leave the spiritual world and I was again in the cave on earth, facing the young man. His eyes looked at me, but he looked like a completely different person now. He was full of tenderness. His lips opened, and he said, "I'm free!"

I instructed him to take off the covenant necklaces and to renounce satan. He did. He received Jesus in his heart and we took him out of that place to be reunited with his mother, who loved him and desired his return.

This experience has been one of the strongest deliverances from captivity that the Lord has allowed me to witness. I have seen many transformed lives as we have taken people out of their prisons. Once delivered, they can begin to live the new lives of freedom that Jesus conquered for them.

I thank God for having taught me this effective way of helping people. I have entered a different level of joy, peace, and victory since finding and destroying the prisons where I myself had been held captive since my childhood.

To Jesus be all the honor and glory for all that He suffered and conquered so that we might be free.

Author's note

In this testimony we see Flory Gonzalez praying for this young man without his permission. It is obvious she was being guided by the Holy Spirit. The truth is, when praying over a major case such as this one, you are never going to get permission to pray by the demonized person. You have to boldly come against the foul spirits, and always under the direction of the Holy Spirit.

To come against major forces of darkness you need to be trained and have the experience that will position you in the level of authority that is necessary to overcome.

It is totally unadvisable to deal with these type of demons if you are a beginner, or have any open doors in your spiritual life.

Chapter 9

Set Free From Homosexuality and Drug Addiction by David Silva Ríos

GUAYAQUIL, ECUADOR

I am from Ecuador and am 30 years old. At the moment, I serve the Lord, my beloved Jesus, in the ministry of intercession and spiritual warfare. Our team's objective is to release people from the captivity in which satan has held them due to iniquity and generational decrees.

The purpose of my testimony is to give glory to my beloved King Jesus. Before knowing Christ, I served the devil in a number of ways: homosexuality, drug addiction, alcoholism, witchcraft, fraud, and many other sins. I do not feel pride in writing this, but I feel it is necessary to share these details so that you might see the fullness of my King's redeeming work.

I grew up in a household of ten people. We lived in total poverty; the devil was determined to destroy us as a family. After torturing my mother and treating her violently, my father left us; I was only two years old. Later, my stepfather came to live with us. He was a very cruel man who mistreated all of us, including my mother. He tried to rape my younger sisters many times.

As a result of this, I grew up with a lot of pain, bitterness, and hatred toward any father figure. On many occasions, we had nowhere to live. We slept in public places and didn't have any way to keep up with our schooling. I remember that we had to go through the trash looking for old shoes so we could go to school. We went hungry and many times, there was only enough food for my youngest brothers and sisters.

All this suffering led me to take refuge in alcohol. I began to drink all kinds of liquor. Once, I was abused sexually. This marked my life and filled me with demons, which took over my physical body, turning it into that of a woman. My entire appearance was feminine. I consumed drugs and entered into homosexual relations with anyone who was available. I became well known for making a scene in public. Everywhere I went, I was surrounded by homosexuals. Then I became involved with rockers. Finally, I ended up with satanists. By this time, I was an adult.

At about this point in my life, a young man who was sent from Heaven offered to help me. I refused. (Today, I realize that God already had a plan in place for my life.) Some days passed and I found myself in a desperate situation. The only solution that occurred to me was suicide. I tried several times, but failed. I felt destroyed and my heart was filled with hatred. I was full of bitterness and resentment from everything that I had gone through.

Early one morning, something made me go out and seek that young man who had offered to help me. He took me to a rehabilitation clinic, where I stayed for two days. The hospital workers belonged to a Christian ministry called "Restoration in Christ." The main pastor took care of me. His name was Carlos Elias Moreira Moreno. He is a servant of God, who has a great love for souls.

My life began to straighten out, thank God, but in the area of homosexuality, I did not find victory. I still wanted to be with men and suffered because I wanted to please God, but couldn't. The homosexual drive was something stronger than my will.

Because of this battle, sometimes the bitterness and hatred that was inside of me would come back, especially against women. In the clinic, they tried to set me free nearly 20 times, but nothing worked. I cried out to God for my freedom when, suddenly, the heavenly Father spoke to me. He told me that He had prepared an encounter with someone who would free me once and for all.

I met a brother who knew about my problems and worked with a ministry that held events throughout the country. He said that Ana Méndez Ferrell was coming to Ecuador with her husband and that he was in charge of those who were helping out for her visit. He said that if I wanted to, he could arrange things so I could see Mr. and Mrs. Ferrell.

They assigned me to the book table. Prophetess Ana Méndez Ferrell approached the stand to give me sales instructions. Suddenly, the Lord spoke to me and said, "This is the woman that I brought for your deliverance." Hallelujah! Praise be to my Eternal Father!

The campaign ended and I went to the hotel where they were staying to render accounts to them. She and her husband were literally from another world. They were full of so much humility and tenderness. A tremendous power emanated from them, but it was not threatening. I was astounded by what I saw and experienced. It was a feeling of peace like I had never felt before. My only thought was that these were God's children and that I wanted to be like them! I settled the accounts and she asked me what I needed. I told her everything and they made an appointment with me for the following day to set me free.

I went back to the hotel with my friend Armando Leon. He is a servant of the Lord who had just been converted at that time. They received me with love and treated me as if I were someone important. They were very attentive to us. I began to explain the dreams that I had and places where the demons had taken me. I told them everything and really let my guard down.

The moment came when Ana told me that I had been held in places of captivity in hell. I wondered if this could be possible. After all, I wasn't dead. I had always thought that you had to have died to be tormented in a place like that. Very gently, she explained everything, showing it to me in the Bible because I was theologically minded and quite religious at the same time.

They began to pray and asked the Father for an angel to help me. He sent two and they could see them. They described the angels, but I didn't believe them. After awhile, my spiritual eyes were opened and I saw them for the first time. Upon seeing something spiritual from God, my body began to tremble. I felt as if I were going to faint. I thought I was going to die. One of the angels touched me and said, "Be encouraged." And in that instant I regained my strength.

They continued to pray. They asked the Father to show them the places of captivity in which I was found. God literally took us to the places where my soul was. They were different regions and jails.

The scariest one that I remember was like a cave where they had me lying on an old wooden table. The place was moldy, hot, and humid. Steam emanated from the walls and the floor. It had the shape of a huge stony heart. I was inside, bound with ropes as thick as those used for ship anchors. These ropes were attached to the floor and embedded in my flesh. They looked very old as they were rusty. There were many demons around the table. One by one, they cut my skin and inserted things inside my body. All of them tormented me. I was seeing in the spiritual realm what I felt in the natural. All the thoughts of hatred, bitterness, pain, and homosexuality were literally the demons that we heard speaking.

Ana asked God the Father to send angels to set me free. She and her husband gave them orders and the angels carried them out. They told the angels to break the ropes and they did it. As each rope broke, I felt it in the natural in my physical body. It was as if they really were embedded in my flesh; it hurt when they came out. I could feel everything that happened.

My friend Armando, who was with me, also saw the captivity. He said it was like they had me on an altar. We were in various places of darkness for about an hour and a half. There were many cells encased in the walls, with rusty bars and a great deal of blood. They took me out from those prisons and places of torment. The angels were always with us, helping us.

Emerson Ferrell noticed that a demon was nailed to my back. He was the guard of my soul. He was assigned to promote lies. When they pulled him off of me, it was like removing the lid from a pot. Hatred, bitterness, pain, desperation, ruin, and poverty all came pouring out. God was removing them all.

Sister Ana, who led the prayer, asked the Lord to take us out of there and take us to heavenly places so that my soul could be established there. The angels held me up because I was very weak. We began to ascend. We passed through a region that looked like a sea. Everything was the color of lead and there were whirlpool-like tunnels in the water. Suddenly, brightness, like that of the sun, appeared and we were absorbed by the light of heavenly places. Everything became beautiful. It was a place full of peace, holiness, purity, and brilliant light.

We returned to the hotel room where we were sitting. Then I saw Jesus. He took the place of my earthly father. He said, *"Forgive Me My son, My beloved David, for letting you down as a boy."* What happened was extremely powerful. I felt my body explode. The Son of God was asking my forgiveness when it was I who had let Him down. I had knifed Him in the face! He then said that He had come to fill me with love. Ana hugged me and enfolded me in love. She was like a person full of light. It was not her, it was Jesus in her. I don't know how to explain it, but it was so real. Then she took the place of my mother and father and asked God to take the iniquity of homosexuality that came from my father.

I have been serving the Lord for six years now. I serve in the same rehabilitation center where they took me. God led us to form a network of intercession in the nation of Ecuador. I am the general coordinator, together with my pastor, of this wonderful team that God put together.

I am under the covering of the man who helped me, Pastor Carlos Elias Moreira Moreno, here in Ecuador. I am also under the apostolic and prophetic covering of the Ferrells.

God has led us in different battles of spiritual warfare to set the places of greatest darkness free in my country. Now we have the Intercessors School where we are training God's army to attack the enemy, to maintain the liberty of territories, and to establish the Kingdom of God upon the earth.

God has also blessed me with my own business. We also watch over different ministries that are under our covering.

This is what God does *because He loves His children.* I give all the glory and honor to Him. The crown is His alone. Hallelujah!

Chapter 10

The Deliverance of Philip
By Dr. Ana Méndez Ferrell

Rescued From Autism, Mental and Physical Deficiency

The powers of darkness are extremely aware of how important it is to affect human beings in infancy. In this time of such fragility, they try to put hooks in children's souls so they can use them later and drag them toward their corrupt plans.

Rose had a high-risk pregnancy. At different times, she suffered blood loss. She and her husband took the authority of Jesus Christ over it and the doctor encouraged them, saying that everything was going to be alright.

Then Philip was born. There were no problems at birth. The boy was beautiful and appeared to be healthy; however, when he was about a year old, they began to notice that he wasn't developing normally. His eyes had a vacant look and he could not hold his head up straight. Every time they gave him solid food, he couldn't swallow it and would spit it out. He had tantrums for no apparent reason.

Little by little, Philip's parents arrived at the conclusion that none of his five senses worked properly. His arms fell limp at his sides, he had no strength, and his legs would not hold him up. He did not produce any sounds when we encouraged him to talk. At his soul level, there was total chaos. It was as though he didn't have feelings and entered states of panic over almost anything. His hypersensitivity and his extreme reactions made daily life very difficult. Philip's capacity to understand was also affected. It seemed that every day brought a different nightmare.

Philip's parents knew they shouldn't lose hope and the Holy Spirit helped them see things through God's eyes. They always spoke blessings over Philip and God's plans for his life. They kept their eyes on the Most High, not allowing the enemy to rob them of the joy of their son, but no matter how hard they tried to persevere in prayer, the defeats were evident.

One day, they heard me speak on "Setting the Captives Free" and were touched by the teaching. They knew that what they were facing with Philip was beyond the scope of the traditional deliverance and divine healing approaches practiced today.

Then they asked us to help them get into the Spirit and see where their little one was being held captive. We agreed, and they proceeded to penetrate the prophetic dimensions. Soon, the Lord manifested on His throne and opened the spiritual realm to begin our search.

The first thing they saw was a room with walls made of blood. There were dead bodies everywhere, but they didn't see Philip. The Lord told them that this was just the entrance and that they had to go in deeper. We arrived at a place where there was a mountain of crevices covered with written generational curses. Philip's father began to ask forgiveness for the iniquity of his ancestors and to cancel the curses. As he prayed, they began to disappear.

The Lord led us to a place full of fleshy membranes that made up some kind of prisons. It was there that we found their son. Part of his spirit was trapped behind these membranes; his father fought like a warrior to get him out of there. As the boy's father, he took authority and commanded that prison to open. He called with great force for Philip to be set free. The membranes began to draw back; it looked like skin was tearing as they began to open.

Then I took the boy spiritually from his cell, but an enormous demon of death came between us. I fought him in a fierce struggle until the power of Jesus gave the victory. The boy came out covered in blood, as though he had been born from that place. Then his father took him in his arms and blessed him as a father would bless his newborn son. They commanded Philip's spirit to integrate with his being and ordered his soul and his body to come into alignment.

The Lord made us understand that during the pregnancy, Philip's spirit had not been able to properly assemble with his soul and body because it had been held captive. He showed us the spirit is designed to fit the soul and body the way a hand fits into a glove. If the spirit does not fill certain areas, they become deflated, much like a balloon with the air let out of it or a glove worn on a hand without fingers. There were parts of Philip's body and soul that were empty; now his freed spirit had to fill them out.

This entire experience was carried out in the Spirit without the boy being present in the house with us; He was visiting with his grandparents. When they brought him home his parents prayed over him to establish everything that happened in the invisible world.

That night he went to bed with no visible change. But the next morning, he awoke crying like a newborn baby. Yet, they began to see accelerated changes: he ate solid food for the first time; he regained his balance; he was able to stand up.

I instructed them to speak Philip's spirit every day and command it to fill his body and soul until there was total victory. As they did so, the Lord showed them that a part of Philip's spirit was asleep, although it was free. They also saw that one part of his brain was connected, while another part was not. They prayed with great power when they saw this and they blew life into his spirit. Suddenly, thousands of glittering particles appeared and began to connect each part of his brain. Emphatically, they declared that the mind of Christ be established in him.

After this, they began to see surprising development in their son month after month. Even the bones of his face changed, giving him the face of a normal child. Today, he plays, laughs, runs, rides a bicycle, and goes to school. He learned to read quickly and enjoys it. His sensitivity that was very unstable became normal. Now, he is a happy, loving, and sociable boy. He is very sweet and has a great sense of humor. The work of God is not complete in him, but they continue to see daily progress.

During this process, Philip's parents have seen the incomparable love of God. They have learned to take the authority that they have in Jesus over every evil spirit in order to cast it out of their lives and the lives of their family. They have appropriated the promises of God for their lives and have paved the way for His miracles to manifest in the lives of their children. They have proclaimed life. God has given them a powerful key, teaching them about prophetic deliverance from captivity. This teaching has definitely touched their lives, Philip's life, and that of their entire family.

To God be the glory.

Chapter 11

My Father's Resurrection by Pastor Joan Manuel Reyes Acosta

OAXACA, MÉXICO

Testimony of the Resurrection of My Father
When the Lord Took Him Out of the Captivity of Death

In September 2004, after returning from Spain, I received a video of Sister Ana Méndez Ferrell titled *Regions of Captivity*. When I saw it, I told the Lord that I would like to experience that kind of power, because I identified with her ministry and teaching. That video helped me to see God in a greater way and to know Jesus' power over death and hell.

On December 28 of that same year, my father was diagnosed with multiple pneumonias and was developing lung cancer. The situation was complicated by the fact that my father was an alcoholic and as a result, suffered from diabetes. We had to hospitalize him and a tube was put inside his lungs because the illness was advancing rapidly.

I prayed. I felt horrible seeing him in such bad shape and I felt helpless, not knowing what to do. Then the Holy Spirit showed me that he was in captivity. That scared me, because I didn't know how to rescue him. I felt that the level of deliverance he needed was beyond me.

Desperate, I left the hospital and decided to watch the video again. The next day I prayed to God, asking for the things that Sister Ana taught to become reality in my father's and my life. I wanted to know how these truths worked.

I determined to enter the ICU (intensive care unit) in the name of Jesus. The doctors were with my father and began to take the tubes out of his mouth. According to them, there was nothing more they could do. This was very hard for me. Yet, full of the Lord's authority, I said, "Jesus Christ came to save the dead and to give them life and life more abundantly and the Lord is more powerful than medical science."

My father's heart beat its last, then, I closed my eyes and began to pray. The Spirit said, "Do it with authority and faith." I did so and declared the Scriptures that I had seen on the video. My voice was no longer mine. The power of the Almighty One issued out of my mouth as I broke the covenants of death that my father had made during his lifetime. Then the Lord said, "I AM that I AM. Do not fear. I am with you. Death is in this room."

When he said this, I felt like an infinite emptiness had opened in the room. It was like being inside of "nothing." It is difficult to explain, but we were in a total void. For the first time in my life, I experienced death. The room filled with a frozen, horrible presence. I felt as though that presence was taking my life. I could barely breathe. I experienced fear and uncertainty. There was total silence as if nothing existed. It was a horrible absence, without life.

Then God said, "Death is in front of you. It is silent, empty and lifeless. It holds the legal rights over your father in its hands and wants to kill him because you have been declaring his salvation. Now raise your prayer and begin to bind that presence just like you saw in the video.

Break the decrees that the enemy has in his hands; those decrees have given him rights over your father since 1945, when your father cursed his parents."

Then I remembered Ana's prayer when she prayed for her friend who was in the hospital; so I said: "I command you satan and the spirit of death to leave in the name of Jesus of Nazareth, the living Christ, you will not take my father to the grave. I declare life to my father and I break the designs, covenants, and decrees that my father made. (He was a Mason grade 28 and a teacher of Masonic literature.)

The Lord added, "Now take him from the captivity of death." In that moment, I saw an angel of the Lord and I saw my father as a child, curled up and crying inside a cell. Jesus continued, "That is a part of his soul that was wounded. Open the door of that prison of death!"

My father could see me. The angel that was with me said, "This is why the Son of Man came, to rescue those who are lost. Now the Son of God is glorified because He descended to hell to take from satan the keys of death and captivity." I was in the Spirit and saw how my father left that prison. I also saw a light surrounding us, full of peace.

In the intensive care room, the picture of death changed. My father's heartbeat came back and stabilized. His respiration became vigorous. I realized that he was getting another opportunity to live in order to set things right with God.

In the experience of taking my father from the regions of death, I realized that many were there because they had cursed their parents and others, in disobedience to the Lord. I asked God's forgiveness for my own past—for failing to esteem Him as Father and for disobeying Him and behaving badly toward my earthly parents.

Something powerful happened within me and I knew I would never be the same. Upon leaving that room, I felt such peace from God. I went home giving glory to Him for what He allowed me to experience in that hospital room. My father was converted to the Lord and was grateful to God for having rescued him from death and for making him His son.

God gave me the victory over death. Since that time, I have taken what I experienced and learned to Oaxaca and to Mexico City. There, we have set many free from the captivity of death and sin.

God allowed me to watch that video without my knowing the magnitude of where it would take me. Today, as God gives us understanding, we minister on captivity and freedom from satanic the designs that hold hundreds of people trapped in the regions of hell. God is even leading us to set cities and nations free, thanks to the teaching that the Lord gave Ana Méndez Ferrell.

I give thanks to Ana for her bravery in confronting darkness. Without that video, I would not have been able to rescue my father from death and hell. Her teaching ministered to me and gave life to the ministry that God gave me.

Ana, my life today is the fruit of this teaching. As the Bible says in Luke 4:18-19: *"The Spirit of the Lord is on me, because He has anointed me to preach good news to the poor. He has sent me to proclaim freedom for the prisoners and recovery of sight for the blind, to release the oppressed, to proclaim the year of the Lord's favor."*

Chapter 12

Can a City Be Born in a Day? by Apostle Fernando Orihuela

La Paz, Bolivia

Rescued From Captivity to See the Glory of God in Potosi, Bolivia

My name is Fernando Orihuela, I serve God in the Apostolic office in La Paz, Bolivia. Along with Dr. Ana Mendez and her husband, Emerson Ferrell, we have done an intensive work in city transformation and spiritual warfare. We have worked together in many nations for almost ten years. This testimony changed my life as I saw the mighty hand of God transforming the hardest and most demonic city in my nation.

It is surprising that the history of Potosi, Bolivia, is so little known throughout the world. It is as though hell itself has tried to erase its ill-fated history so that the consequences of its wickedness can continue to be transmitted unnoticed from generation to generation.

The enemy wanted to keep Potosi's history a mystery because he knows it plays an important role in its spiritual condition. So, I will begin by sharing some of Potosi's historical background.

Around 1535, Spain was rife with internal struggles. Peru and northern Argentina were still unknown territories. Years prior, one of the last descendants of the Inca king, Huaina Capac, was told about the discovery of a fantastic mountain, which held an extraordinary treasure of silver of rare quality within it. Around 1545, Captain Juan de Villarroel and other Spaniards discovered it and began its exploitation.

Beginning in April of that year, Potosi became an important mining town. Thanks to the silver, it grew with breathtaking speed, becoming the largest city of the Americas in 1650, with more inhabitants than London and Paris. Its influence was known throughout Europe.

The riches extracted from the mountain became a magnet for many people. For example, the Argentinean writer Raul Molina in his book "Historia de rio de la Plata" (*History of the Silver River)*, called it the "Mecca of Spanish commerce of that time."[1]

THE PRICE OF EXPLOITATION

How was such exploitation possible? What was the price for sending such tremendous wealth to the Iberian Peninsula?

Miners paid a very high price for the production of silver. Some historians have estimated that, in a little over 350 years, 12 million men died extracting the silver in this part of America. The mining methods were deadly. The population was so heavily decimated that Spain needed to import African slaves. However, due to the geography and extreme cold, the slaves could not survive for more than a year.

THE "HOLY LEAF"

The city of Potosi is located 4,017 meters (about 13,200 feet) above sea level. In order to work the mines at this altitude, the miners chewed coca leaves to help invigorate them. This was an existing practice of the Inca people. This, of course, produced drug addiction.

When the Spaniards arrived in America and discovered the properties of coca, they introduced it as a vital part of the exploitation process. The consumption of cocaine replaced eating, eliminated the will to fight, and turned the men into little less than machines. Each one of them could work close to 36 continuous hours, without needing to eat or sleep.

However, after a few months, the results were tragic. The men were emaciated and malnourished, and their lungs were consumed by the acids they breathed in the mines. They saw alcohol as a way to escape their suffering. Until the beginning of the twenty-first century, Potosi was characterized as the only city in Bolivia with negative growth and a life expectancy of less than 47 years.

When the "silver fever" ended, the city became a desolate place. Her former glory disappeared. The origin of riches for all of Europe, where an entire continent earned their living, simply disappeared.

THE PRESENCE OF SHADOWS

One of the practices that appeared in the Bolivian mines is called "The Uncle worship." The Uncle is a representation of the devil, to whom sacrifices and offerings are frequently made.

The reason is simple: it is believed that the devil is the owner of the mine's riches and its only authority. This belief has contaminated nearby cities. Christianity has not grown in these regions after more than 100 years of preaching. In this city, typical characteristics of those who have been given to idolatry are manifest, such as unbelief, indifference, occult practices, and poverty. Spiritual fortresses govern the city and the Freemasons have also left their mark. This is only a sample of the tremendous spiritual problems facing Potosi.

MY FIRST CONTACT WITH THE CITY

When I traveled to Potosi for the first time in 1995, I could verify some notable aspects of it. It was very difficult to expect to have any spiritual impact or to establish any form of spiritual warfare or group deliverance. My own experience trying to deliver someone in that city was hard and required lots of effort and divine power. You could feel the oppression and demonic control everywhere. The churches were small and made few converts every year. The authority and influence of the Catholic Church (a mix of Romanism and native cultures) was visible and what little remained of economic activity still depended upon the colossal mountain of silver, which had long since seen its glory days.

The leadership of the Christian Church was divided; it was extremely difficult for Christian leaders to talk about working together for any length of time. During a time of intercession, our team received insight that Potosi was a blood altar, probably one of the highest on earth. It was undoubtedly the altar with the greatest number of lives sacrificed upon it.

My first job was to try to bring together the leaders of the city. With God's help and a pair of pastor friends, I succeeded in having a first meeting, during which I proposed evangelizing the city. Of the 95 churches in the city, 90 were present. It was a great success. After holding Communion, we began to plan what would prove to be the greatest mobilization of the Church in our history. The date set for the event was May 2001.

DIVINE CONTACTS

All of this work took close to five years (and many breaking experiences). The final months prior to the event were especially intense. In January of that year, God allowed me to meet Ana Méndez Ferrell. We were both invited to an event in Denver, Colorado. God allowed me to tell her the vision. After a long conversation, she felt in her spirit to accept our invitation and to participate in the taking of Potosi. I was also able to contact Brother Hector Torres, beloved friend and renowned writer and speaker.

The strategy was simple. The evangelism would take a week, open to every church and with massive publicity. We wanted to impact close to

25,500 homes, visiting them one by one. We also needed to do a spiritual assault, "binding the strong man." This would be accomplished a week prior. It would be a closed event with the participation of no more than 70 intercessors.

THE VEIL PARTED

During our five-year period of preparation for the two-week initiative, we traveled nearly every month and a half to do an intense study of the city. We did spiritual mapping and visited every museum and place of idolatry. We also entered the mines and sought every possible trace of the one who was spiritually "guilty" of this entire disaster. In spite of all that research, if you had asked me who the strong man of Potosi was, I would not have known how to answer your question.

Ana Méndez Ferrell had barely arrived in Potosi when she called on a smaller group for a meeting. After a few brief comments, we entered a very special time of intercession. I was not prepared for what happened. For more than three hours, the Lord allowed us to have an experience like I had never had before. Angels appeared among us, and they took us to spiritual places where the city was held captive.

It is one thing to know the Bible and settle doubts about a place or region with the help of a dictionary. I knew how to do that well, thanks to my theological education. However, it's another thing to *be* in those spiritual places and to actually *see them*, face to face.

MEETING THE QUEEN OF HEAVEN

We learned that the Queen of Heaven, in the form of a large dragon, was the jailer of the city. This is one of the most powerful rulers in satan's kingdom and is the strongest feminine deity in all the pagan religions. She rules under different names such as Isis in Egypt, Ishtar in Babylon, Asera and Astarot among the Philistines, Diana of the Ephesians, the Black Madonna, Guadalupe, and all of the virgins that are just a disguise of the Roman and Greek goddesses and many others. The list is too long to mention all of them.

As we prayed over the city, past and present mixed together in images that were alive. So much pain, so much harm had been committed against the earth and against Potosi. We could hear creation groaning to be set free.

We could hear the sound of all the blood shedding linked to pain and iniquity as we earnestly interceded. Thankfully, angels came to assist us. Our prayer took a higher dimension in the spirit realm. We were able to see all the structures of evil over the city along with the horrible covenants that kept it captive. As we released the power of God over our enemy we saw chains being broken and covenants destroyed. This was an amazing experience that I could only describe as the apostle Paul said, "... *whether in the body or out of the body, I do not know...*" (see 2 Cor. 12:3). I only know what I "saw," and it was real.

In that time of intercession, we understood that the spirit of the Queen of Heaven had taken the blood of those millions of men in the mines in order to establish her throne. This throne had two powerful spiritual elements: one was the fact that it was in a very high place, the top of the mountain overseeing Potosi is close to 5,300 meters, or about 17,400 feet above sea level; the second was the fact that the blood of these victims was shed in an almost ritualistic manner.

The spiritual guardians of the Queen of Heaven are usually Mammon (riches) and Death. It was evident that these two principalities had openly manifested in the city.

After we fought along with God's angels to deliver the city, the Spirit of the Lord led us to restore the city and the land. We prayed for the blood of Christ to cover it and for the generational pain to be healed.

At a certain point, the Lord led us to take Potosi out of captivity from the scary spiritual dungeons that had held it prisoner for generations. Afterward, we declared that the riches of the nation were being freed.

Just months after this prayer initiative, immense deposits of natural gas were discovered in our country.

Only five people participated in this high-level warfare, which took place in three sessions. In each of them, something broke, and we saw signs in the heavens.

In one of them we saw the spirit of occult over the city, it had the appearance of a huge ape who cast spells on the inhabitants to make them captives. As in the previous case, God's angels helped us break their influence, and we opened the prisons. It was beautiful to see them set free after so many years of oppression.

THE PRISON DOORS ARE OPENED

After the last intercession, something amazing happened. The people began to come to Christ all by themselves, one by one. There were times when a group would approach our team, requesting prayer and wanting to know the Lord. One whole community of farmers asked for someone to visit their community because everyone there had received Jesus in their heart. The evangelistic mobilization began. More than 400 evangelists were sent to the streets to conduct home visits. Evangelism teams worked using music and dramas, movies were shown in the different town squares, we held meetings in movie theaters and offered free medical care to the needy. God was visiting Potosi.

In a little over ten days of evangelism, there were 40,790 decisions for Christ. This was unprecedented. In the second day alone, the supply of 17,000 decision cards (which had been prepared by the city's team of pastors) ran out. People received the Lord even after midnight, in the middle of winter, at minus 11 degrees Celsius (12.2 degrees Fahrenheit). Inmates, city authorities, students, and thousands of children received the Lord.

The captivity of Potosi was destroyed. Thanks to the leading of the Holy Spirit, the whole city came out to freedom and the people automatically came to Jesus. It is just as simple as that.

LATER CONSEQUENCES

Three months after the assault, the nation's president, who lead the country in corruption, resigned. A few months later, he died, afflicted by a terminal illness. The most influential political parties of the previous 50 years disappeared along with him. The Lord's explanation was very simple, *"The invisible government fell. [Therefore,] the visible government falls."*

In just three years' time, Potosi obtained second place in the nation in economic and investment projections. Urban development was visible. Even the local soccer team won a place in the famous *Conquerors of America* championship—for the first time in its history. The city pastors continue praying together frequently, holding prayer walks. The hiring of children to work in the mines has been prohibited by law. Glory to God! The Lord is doing something there. Surely Potosi still needs much prayer and help, but one thing is undeniable: a visible transformation of the community has begun.

"Can a nation be born in a day?" asked the prophet (Isaiah 66:8).

"Yes, it is possible!" I declare it, because I have seen it.

ENDNOTE

1.   Buenos Aires: Ediciones de la Municipalidad, 1949.